Sightings
a collection of poetry
with an Essay, 'Communicating Poems'
Gillian Bickley
Proverse Hong Kong

In **Sightings: a collection of poetry with an Essay, "Communicating Poems"**, supported by the Hong Kong Arts Development Council, academic turned full-time writer and editor Gillian Bickley invites the reader to share her enjoyment of city and country, simple and complex ideas and events, and her empathy with the largely innocent people she has come across. In her trademark transparent style, she draws on events, happenings, creatures, artefacts and objects she has seen, and on places and people she has experienced in Asia, Europe, North America and Africa, as well as on stimulating and memorable books she has read. In strongly contrasting mood, a final sequence of poems, taken from a long novel in progress, sketches a chronological narrative, alive with complex emotions, concluding in a form of quiet acceptance.

In 'Communicating Poems', she considers the practicalities of addressing both local and global audiences in a single edition of poetry, taking as examples her first two poetry collections, **Moving House and other Poems from Hong Kong** and **For the Record and Other Poems of Hong Kong**. She has expanded and revised this essay from a talk she gave at a University Seminar and now invites feedback from readers on the ideas presented in it.

Supported by

The Hong Kong Arts Development Council fully supports freedom of artistic expression. The views and opinions expressed in this project do not represent the stand of the Council.

Sightings

a collection of poetry

with an Essay, 'Communicating Poems'

Gillian Bickley

Proverse Hong Kong

Sightings: a collection of poetry, with an Essay, 'Communicating Poems'
by Gillian Bickley.
2nd paperback ed., published in Hong Kong by Proverse Hong Kong, November 2016.
Copyright © Proverse Hong Kong, November 2016.
ISBN: 978-988-8228-54-6.
Available from: https://www.createspace.com/6647719

1st published in pbk in Hong Kong by Proverse Hong Kong, 2007.
Copyright © Proverse Hong Kong, 17 May 2007.
ISBN 978-988-99668-1-2

Enquiries:
Proverse Hong Kong, P.O. Box 259, Tung Chung Post Office, Hong Kong SAR.
E-mail: proverse@netvigator.com Website: proversepublishing.com

The right of Gillian Bickley to be identified as the author of this work has been asserted by her in accordance with the Copyright, Designs and Patents Act 1988.
The right of Marion Bethel to be identified as the author of 'Foreword', of Harry Guest to be identified as the author of 'Preface', of Ma Kwai Hung to be identified as the author of 'Introduction' has been asserted by each of them respectively in accordance with the Copyright, Designs and Patents Act 1988.

Page design by Proverse Hong Kong. Cover design by Kevin Kwok.
Cover photograph by and © Proverse Hong Kong.

Poems from Gillian Bickley, *For the Record and other Poems of Hong Kong,* Proverse Hong Kong, 2003 and Gillian Bickley, *Moving House and other Poems from Hong Kong*, Poverse Hong Kong, 2005, are included with permission of the copyright holders.

All rights reserved. No part of this publication may be reproduced, stored in a retrieval system, or transmitted, in any form or by any means, electronic, mechanical, photocopying, recording or otherwise, without the prior written permission of the publisher or author. The book is sold subject to the condition that it shall not, by way of trade or otherwise, be lent, re-sold, re-presented, hired out or otherwise circulated without the publisher's prior written consent in any form of binding or cover other than that in which it is published and without a similar condition including this condition being imposed on the subsequent owner or purchaser.
The copyright holders would be delighted to give written permission (including but not restricted to republishing, inclusion in anthologies, translation, reading, performance and use as set pieces in examinations and festivals) to use Gillian Bickley's poems.
Please request, in writing, any and all permissions from Proverse Hong Kong.

British Library Cataloguing in Publication Data (for 1st edition)

Bickley, Gillian
Sightings : a collection of poetry ; with an essay,
'Communicating poems'
1. English poetry - China - Hong Kong - 21st century -
History and criticism
I. Title
821.9'14

ISBN-13: 9789889966812

Introduction

Sightings is a poetry collection by Gillian Bickley, who was born and educated in the United Kingdom and has lived in Hong Kong since 1970. Gillian Bickley has already published two other books of poetry, namely, *For the Record and other Poems of Hong Kong* and *Moving House and other Poems from Hong Kong*.

Living in Hong Kong is perhaps too demanding for most people to take a good look at their surroundings, as well as to feel and think about the place. People are lost in the hustle and bustle of this extremely busy and commercialized city. *Sightings* is a collection of poems that inspires us to slow down, to move at a calmer pace and to taste the sense of the city. Apart from focusing only on the skyscrapers and the things that Hong Kong is famous for, Gillian Bickley has looked into other aspects that we often fail to notice in our daily life. This collection takes a step further beyond the sights and sounds of the city we live in.

Gillian has used different poetic tones and moods, and comparisons of various cultures and current world issues to emphasise the feelings and thoughts of the people. She has made use of everyday life situations and turned them into life lessons. She has also tactfully infused in the poems sayings that we are familiar with, such as "The glass—as we know—is half-way full or half-way empty". Her own experiences are reflected in the poems and help draw us closer to her.

This collection of poems sets out to leave an imprint of feeling and understanding in our minds. Every poem weaves a different story and situation, but always strives to remind readers that, apart from the busy-ness of the city, there are other aspects that we should consider.

Gillian Bickley has yet again amazed readers with her beautiful poetry, and we look forward for more to come.

Introduction

   Besides the poems, there is an extra section, "Communicating Poems", which is based on a lecture given by the author to students and teachers. This section will be found extremely useful by those readers who are interested in reading or writing poems. There is also a questionnaire related to this, for readers to complete so as to give Gillian some feedback, and to facilitate interaction between the author and her readers.

Ma Kwai Hung
Examiner
Hong Kong Arts Development Council
December 2006

Preface

Do men and women write poetry differently? If Sappho's fragments were unattributed, would a reader guess her gender? We tend to say that Emily Dickinson and the eighteenth-century Japanese poet Chiyo display a "feminine sensibility", but does in fact this merely mean that each writes with a sharpened delicacy and from a totally idiosyncratic viewpoint?

Gillian Bickley walks around the world with her eyes open, relishing the phenomena she passes as she makes fresh connections between a teacher and a road-sweeper or, seeing a small boy on the back seat of a car, leaves an enjoyable and enigmatic question-mark in the reader's mind – because she herself will never know the next move time will take.

The most impressive poems in this book are "Warm Comfort" and "Roman Stones". In the first she examines attitudes to death and the after-life over the millennia and, criticising those who "place the letters of the alphabet / and a tumbler on a table", remarks simply of the dead

> When we need them, they will come.

In the second, again using a historical perspective, she employs a richer palette then elsewhere since, in a museum in Chester, we are shown

> The smiling faces of the dead as they recline,
> raising in one hand their final, eternal glass of wine.

A cool Christian focus, urging us to recall "the blessings of this life" in "Art is Long" and "The Purpose of Praise", also asks about "heartbreak in heaven" and, in "Creating Words", faces those "intertwined thoughts" which assist us beyond the horror of Good Friday.

There is a subdued wit in "Unstained" and "Innocent

Preface

Solidarity". The beautifully observed "Token" offers a delicate instruction to attend to the world around us. In "Balance", the close and the far are juxtaposed in a surrealist way so that a distant helicopter and a nearby bird are the same size – the way in "City Golf Club" pompom chrysanthemums are compared with golf-balls, reminding one of a painting by Paul Nash.

"Parish Priest" and "Walking Stick" are affectionate character-sketches lending the two men three dimensions. The second poem about her father again wonders wryly about the tangibility of heaven. When Gillian Bickley can compose and organize poems as tellingly as these it is somewhat to be regretted that she didn't "work" more at some of her aperçus which, although often either amusing or original, stay prosaically as diary-jottings rather than as full-blown poems.

Does one detect a feminine approach? There are more exclamation-marks than a male writer would use (!) and perhaps "Her Choice" indicates an intenser possibility of identification. Otherwise, no. This is not the work of a "poetess", an outdated word which tended to be used disparagingly. There are real poems in this collection which would be welcome in many contemporary anthologies.

Harry Guest
Honorary University Fellow
University of Exeter
United Kingdom
February 2007

Sightings: a collection of poetry
with an Essay, 'Communicating Poems'

Table of Contents

Introduction by Ma Kwai Hung		5
Preface by Harry Guest		7
Table of Contents		9
Illustration Acknowledgement		12
Author's Acknowledgements		13
Foreword by Marion Bethel		15

Events and Encounters

1	Art is Long	21
2	Super-ego	23
3	Optimism	24
4	The Purpose of Praise	25
5	Country Walk	26
6	Humble Indignation	27
7	Take up your Bed and Walk!	28
8	Innocent Solidarity	29
9	Hallowe'en	30
10	Stranger and Stranger	31
11	A Fine Sense of Courtesy	32
12	Old Accounts	33
13	"Take care what you wish for!"— The cost of a wish	34
14	Squirreling	35
15	Parents and Children	36
16	Always a Child	37
17	Politically Correct?	38
18	Unstained	39
19	Western Fung Shui Practitioner	40
20	The Value of Information	41
21	Permission	42
22	Stiff Upper Lip	43
23	Divine Discontent: an essay in Logic	44

24	Parish Priest	45
25	Walking Stick	46
26	Warm Comfort	47
27	Publication	51
28	Cities of the Mind	52
29	Gift from an Astronaut	53
30	Transit Lounge	54

Sightings with Mis-Communications

31	Token	56
32	Doubt	57
33	Too Much Reality	58
34	In-fin-ity	59
35	Cutting H[edge]	60
36	Shampoo Lady	61
37	Ambiguous Advertising	61
38	Ambiguous Praise: Flying High	61
39	Difficult to Do	61
40	Fashion Sense	62
41	Curtains for Some	63
42	Civil Contract, Hong Kong	64
43	Balance	65
44	White Flags	66
45	Fragile Symbols	67
46	Battle Sight	68
47	Asphalt Flower	69
48	Christmas Bear [-hug]	70
49	Leaves: Street Sweeper & Teacher Compared	71
50	Differences	72
51	Mediterranean Reaction	73
52	First Impressions	74
53	Disappearing Harbour	75
54	Coffin Play	76
55	Rowboat	77
56	Spectacles	78
57	Images	79
58	Sweet Provider	80

59	Thoughtfulness	81
60	"City Golf Club"	82
61	Her Choice	83
62	Aperçus	87
63	What Bird Flew?	91
64	The Watcher Watched	92
65	Young Master	93
66	Is there Heartbreak in Heaven?	94
67	Creating Words	95
68	Roman Stones	97

From a Novel, in progress

69	Illusions	100
70	Deserts	101
71	Butterfly (dramatic monologue)	102
72	Labels	106
73	She would have been here	107
74	Favour	108
75	Cold Dawning	109
76	Shelter, Foetus	110
77	Brief Bloom	112
78	The Visit	115

Communicating Poems	117
About the Author and her Work	133
Notes	135
From Advance Comments and Reviews of Published Poetry by Gillian Bickley	145

Illustration Acknowledgement

Cover photo by Gillian Bickley edited by Kevin Kwok "Buddy Bear" street sculpture, seen in Nathan Road, Tsim Sha Tsui, Kowloon, Hong Kong, March 2006

Acknowledgements

Author's Acknowledgements

Without my husband, Verner Bickley, I might not now be sited where I am, would not sight and experience many of the people and places that I do. His own love of books provides a fruitful domestic collegiality out of which doubtless come some of the citations that I make. I am grateful to him also for his judicious and patient editorial input.

At Hong Kong Baptist University, colleagues in the English Department organized and participated in the Staff Seminar at which the talk was given, the basis for the essay, "Communicating Poems". I am also grateful for continued assistance from Professor Chung Ling, Dean of the Faculty of Arts, Professor Terry Yip of the Department of English, Mr S. H. Tong and Mr Henry So of ITSC, and Mr Danny K. C. Chow.

The energy and organizing power of the group of Hong Kong poets and supporters, meeting monthly under the name, "OutLoud", the monthly arabic *nadwah* (literary gathering), and the activities of the Hong Kong Writers' Circle and the Hong Kong Women in Publishing group all provide an ongoing and valuable context for testing new writing and ideas, gaining new knowledge, and extending skills. The Hong Kong International Literary Festival provides annual stimulation.

The Hong Kong media have been generous in running features and reviews and airing interviews and readings.

The Royal Asiatic Society (Hong Kong Branch) and numerous Departments and Centres at various Hong Kong universities all provide opportunities for extending understanding and knowledge of our position in the world.

The support of the Hong Kong Arts Development Council is also much appreciated.

In his Introduction, Mr Ma Kwai Fong, Hong Kong Arts Development Council Examiner, consciously expresses his

Acknowledgements

view of how Hong Kong people may view my work.

Marion Bethel, prize-winning Bahamian poet and writer, who visited Hong Kong in 2006 as a guest writer at the International Writers' Workshop at Hong Kong Baptist University discusses this collection, *Sightings*, in the context of international writing.

Harry Guest, United Kingdom based poet, translator, compiler and critic, with many years experience, living and teaching in Asia, debates the question, considering *Sightings*, whether there are any differences between how women and men write poetry.

I thank all three for their generous support in giving their time and attention and for their kind and useful observations.

Finally, I thank all the people of Hong Kong, as well as visitors to Hong Kong, who, collectively and variously, in the present and through the past, provide a stimulating environment, intellectually and visually.

Foreword

In October and November 2006, I was one of the eight guest international writers who participated in the Hong Kong Baptist University's annual International Writers' Workshop. I first met Gillian Bickley at the Welcoming Reception and Dinner, when we talked about her work as a former professor of English at the University and also her life as a poet, biographer, historian, essayist and publisher. We met again at the Hong Kong Festival Fringe Club at one of the readings organized under the name, "OutLoud", when I read a few of my poems.

Later, in early November 2006, Gillian invited me and a fellow writer at the Workshop, Funso Aiyejina of Nigeria, on a Walking Tour of Colonial Hong Kong conducted by herself. I was particularly interested in understanding something of this aspect of Hong Kong's history in light of my own country's former status as a British colony. It was during this three hour tour and the following lunch at the Hong Kong Jockey Club that I experienced Gillian's passion and love for her adopted home, Hong Kong. I was struck not only by her commitment to recording subjects in the colonial history of Hong Kong, its culture, traditions and contemporary life, but also by her facility with employing the various genres of writing in realizing this commitment.

This collection of poems, fittingly called "Sightings", plays skillfully on the homophonic words 'sight' and 'site' in each poem. Whether the poet is viewing the landscape of the mind, emotions, or the physical and human environs of Hong Kong, she communicates her own unique vision and insight or gillianesque way of looking at or considering an event or encounter. At whatever site she chooses to express her lyrical voice, we experience the poet's feelings travelling from the senses, in particular the sense of sight, to the passions, struggling always to express what words,

Foreword

when poetically framed, can say about our interior selves and external life.

In Bickley's work we share the struggle, the insight and the discovery of the poet in her encounters, not merely the reportage of what the eye sees in a physical sense. In each poem we come away with a sense of the poet's enduring link to life in Hong Kong and her compassion for each human being on whom she reflects. In "Take up your Bed and Walk!" the poet meets a disabled old man and reflects on the biblical story of the lame man who was healed from his sickness through grace. During this current encounter the poet re-considers whether or not an instant miracle actually occurred in the ancient story. Sensing that no miracle is imminent for this old man, the poet manages to articulate, in any case, her sincere and honest wish of good health and prosperity for him.

Reading Bickley's poems reminded me of a poem by the Caribbean poet Lorna Goodison (b. 1947), from Jamaica, called "Come Let Your Eyes Feel":

> Come let your eyes feel
> the colours, the landscape
> of Heartease[1]
> the long day will pass
> drawn lightly through rays
> of African Star grass
> and at night a bed-tranquil
> borrowed from rest
> and pillows all peaceful
> an heart's ease is this.

Both poets, Bickley and Goodison, experience and claim the eye as an emotion and give it the capacity to feel. The American poet Wallace Stevens (1879-1955), in his poem "Examination of the Hero in a Time of War", frames the eye in exactly this way:

Foreword

> The hero is a feeling, a man unseen
> As if the eye was an emotion
> As if in seeing we saw our
> feeling
> In the object seen....

In *Sightings* Bickley hones in on an event or encounter, feels her way through the sighting and produces a compelling journey for the reader. It is, indeed, the feeling eye, the compassionate and insightful eye of the poet, which enables us to travel the landscapes, both physical and human, of Hong Kong and other places. This eye offers us vignettes and anecdotes that raise both metaphysical and ethical questions.

One of Bickley's metaphysical themes is the tension between being and death. There are numerous poems, such as "Coffin Play" and "Rowboat", which address the issue of death largely through the lens of a Christian cosmology, with references to Greek mythology. In "Warm Comfort" the poet explores various traditions and responses in regard to death, grave sites and epitaphs. This poem is intense throughout and surprising in its ending. It reads, in part,

> The dead are not like us
> because they are dead.
> ...
> "Here lies one who longed to die", we read.
> But ...
> such singleness of mood
> is something we may not want,
> at least not every day,
> not in our living days.

Bickley's poems are also marked by a strong ethical sense and a constant and engaging lyricism that sustains her expression. The poet brings her Anglo-European heritage to bear in her poems with many allusions to western mythology, traditions and sensibility. As an English-speaking poet she writes within that literary tradition but

Foreword

she also writes with a sense of place and her own unique perspective on being a belonger in Hong Kong. In "Civil Contract, Hong Kong", the sighting of a white pigeon in between two colonial buildings on Old Bailey Street compels the poet to question the social contract concerning life in Hong Kong.

Having read *Sightings* I understand more fully the capacity and power of poetry, perhaps more so than any other genre, to allow a poet to lay claim in a proprietary way to the world in which she lives.

A remarkable quality of some of Bickley's poems such as "Curtains for Some" is the sense of playfulness on the poet's part as she considers aspects of popular culture. Again in this poem it is the roving and razor sharp eye that enables us to see and feel the irony and humour in this encounter. In the second stanza the poet says,

> Strangely, in the middle
> of fake medieval tapestries
> and rich brocades
> Mickey Mouse cushions grin.

Bickley's body of work in *Sightings* causes me to consider lastly Wallace Stevens's poem, "A Postcard from the Volcano", in which he states in the third stanza,

> And least will guess that with our bones
> We left much more, left what still is
> The look of things, left what we felt
>
> At what we saw.

Bickley's poems manifest her intention to allow her gaze, her trained and poetic eye, to capture the sights, insights and sites of being and dying and freeze-frame them for the record. The generations-to-come will then know that **this poet left what she felt at what she saw**. And we come to know that because of her labour of love in recording the

Foreword

lyrics of life, this poet's soul and heart will come to rest at ease **at night a bed-tranquil.**

Marion Bethel
Nassau
The Bahamas
February 2007

Events and Encounters

Events and Encounters

Art is Long

"Art is long, but life is short"
the Preacher, Ecclesiastes,[2] said,
thousands of years ago.

And when you read out this passage,
in Church, a decade ago,
you gave it such emphasis . . .!

And I saw our friend smile and agree
and understand why you did so.

And it is true, of course,
particularly for people like us,
whose work and joy
is in books and thoughts,
music and art,
and graciousness in people,

that we need to remember
our own and others'
mortality.

The glass — as we know — is
half-way full
or half-way empty.

The Preacher's emphasis,
I think, is not that life is
unfairly short.

Events and Encounters

— We can never
perfect our own art; nor
experience and learn
from all the work
of the world's myriad others. —

But that, though life *is* short,
art survives.

We can survive
through what we produce.

The sum of human art
carries us — all of us —
forward, ever in its arms, in its progress;
whether our own
small speck
of a contribution remains
distinct, or not.

And it also carries this message:

"In pursuit of art,
which will live,
whatever we do or do not do,

don't let us forget
to live our life,
which only we can do,
which only we have been given."

June 2004

Events and Encounters

Super-ego[3]

It takes time to search in memory
for stored parts of me,
not used for a long time.

There may be interference:
the questions,
"Is it wise?
"Why should I?"
and, "Should I?"

Are those parts good, or useful,
or even <u>allowed</u>
by the super-ego I have grown (not quite like a shell;
not quite like a jail)?

But, questioning solved,
the address successfully searched,
I find they are still here.

1982; revised, Summer 2006

Events and Encounters

Optimism

Ever since I heard someone say,
"The normal human condition is misery",
I have felt quite cheerful.

Every time I tend to depression,
I remember this sentence
and retrieve
my equanimity.

We are told that,
in the Middle Ages,[4]
men gallivanted
in the face of plague,
the death of children,
and a host of grinning memento mori —
carved or painted human skeletons,
which prefigured their, and still prefigure our, own death.

Maybe the gloom and all those skulls
had the same effect on them,
as this example of a friend's
attempt at wisdom had on me:

suggesting the occasionally appealing philosophy
of accepting — but not necessarily expecting —
the worst, as ones lot.
1982; revised, Summer 2006

Events and Encounters

The Purpose of Praise

God invented Praise
to serve man,
not God.

How can He,
removed and above all things,
greasily rub his stomach,
gustily inhale
the smoke of meaty sacrifices,
jealously desire
complex man's few
simple thoughts of pleasure
to lie beating at his feet?

No. In sympathy for man
and loving-kindness
for his life of torture,
he requires this duty from him.
(Men do things for duty, otherwise undone.)

"Praise me in all created things," He says.
"Spare time,
out of your anguish,
the burden of impossible decisions;
consciously attempt
to take pleasure, every day,
every moment,
if you can.

"It helps
a little."

1982; revised, Summer 2006

Events and Encounters

Country Walk

Green leaves soak city-dwellers,
drawn into the concrete dust
of their daily diet;
oiling their parched skins.

Cool streams,
running over rocks, set in ferns,
wash dulled ears,
penetrate with joy.

Perfumed white stars,
dank wood and rotting leaves
make thin blood soar.

Soft tendrils' grope,
sharp prickles' whip,
smooth hot rocks' slap:

all infuse our bodies
with life;
and all the country walk
restores our bone-dried,
paper-packed minds
to lively sense.

1982; revised, Summer 2006

Events and Encounters

Humble Indignation

Written after seeing a Chinese gentleman standing in the open air, near the Hong Kong Court of Final Appeal, with a message around his neck. I supposed that he might have been a member of one of the families with a handicapped child, accused of receiving too much publicly funded assistance and then suddenly asked to pay back the overpayment. The response of some of the families was, that they themselves had reported the matter to the Government Department concerned, quite some time previously, but that there had been no previous response. They objected to being cast as grasping and dishonest, through no fault of their own.

Head bowed, quietly intense,
you stand with your story
hanging, posted around your neck
in bold black Chinese characters.

Not defiant, but wanting
to tell us your pain,
your indignation
at being so misunderstood,
so betrayed, so demeaned,
so treated not as our fellow.

I wish I could understand
your written message
and tell you, at least,
that I feel sorry.

October 2005

Events and Encounters

Take up your Bed and Walk!

The frail old man, blue jumpered,
face becoming skull,
crept along,
pushing his wheel chair.
It had a red cushion on the seat,
decorated
with a Chinese character.

If it said, "Long life!"
I hope it also wished him,
"good health!" and at least a
degree of prosperity.

— I always thought that the man
stricken with a palsy
leapt up
and could stride away,
when Jesus said,
"Take up thy bed and walk!"[5]

But perhaps he also
effortfully and slowly
jerked and heaved to his feet,
stood up tremblingly and weak,
and took
long months
really to walk again,
as he had walked before.

October 2005

Events and Encounters

Innocent Solidarity

A very wide man
held the hand
of a wider, very wide man
as they walked
down
the steps
outside
a narrow, tall, high-rising tower.

Was it for comfort, for company?

For safety, perhaps?

— "Don't let's fall here!
Shall we hold hands,
to be sure?"

We see their simple friendship
— in middle age —
their innocent
solidarity.

This is the way
the extremely horizontally challenged
find their way,
through an excessively alien, vertical dimension.

December 2005

Events and Encounters

Hallowe'en

"This Friday", he said, "Haaah Low Een".

Did I look like a witch then?

Did my three-piece,
navy, business trouser suit
and two BLACK bags with long handles and wheels,
which I walked like grumbling dogs,
dragging them behind me,
seem to him an urban version of a sharp-nosed
woman with wild hair, on a broomstick, near the moon,
and a black *cat* next to her?

Or had he been puzzling for days
on this very strange word; and so jumped
at the chance that my riding high with him gave
— in a lift at the Center, 99 Queen's Road,
Hong Kong, SAR, China —
to be linguistically informed?

"Yes, I said, 'Hallowe'en'"

"Haaah Low Een", he said again,
shrugging as he struggled
with the strange
difficulties
that the English language
posed. . . . "Haaah Low Een".

Experienced and written, 25 October 2005

Events and Encounters

Stranger and Stranger

He walked
swingingly
down the road,
opening his mouth
and bulging his tongue
out and up,
as if troubled by a hair
he could not remove.

I, standing at the bus stop,
watched him,
while scrunching
abdominal muscles,
to reduce flab.

Did we look
<u>equally</u> odd
to any others,
who might be watching
us <u>both</u>?

3 November 2005

Events and Encounters

A Fine Sense of Courtesy

Courtesy comes in many forms.
Some bus drivers hoot their horns,
indignant that people choose to dash
across the road against the lights.

But you, driver
of Champion Cleaning Transport Company,
you just glanced at the red man
and smiled when I glanced at him, too,
and stopped at the kerb, stepping back.

Mrs Beeton,[6] also,
had a fine sense of courtesy;
instructing wives of the new Victorian middle class,
when kissing their husband,
on his morning's way to work,
to hand him his hat and gloves
but glance at his umbrella,

allowing <u>him</u> judgement and choice!

Completed, June 2006

Events and Encounters

Old Accounts

Quite affluent people, surprisingly,
talk quite a lot, about what small things cost —
flexing their brains perhaps,
in an ample, but boring, retirement.

Not for them,
the daily crossword puzzle
of the merely intellectual.

Do we ever pause,
to think, how much
each action and word,
every thought, expunges
from our limited portion of life?

Some geniuses die young.
— And so do the good, they say. —

The life force used
in reaching such heights of perfection
is clearly extraordinarily great.

But the volume of vigour required,
piling up profits,
it seems,
is quite a bit less.

If you want to live long,
then, aspire to be rich,
not great!

Edited from notes, August 2006

Events and Encounters

"Take care what you wish for!"
—The Cost of a Wish

Wishes <u>can</u> be granted.

When your friend's daughter
bought a bungalow
out in the country,
you panicked. You thought
of the empty days,
with no-one to chat to,
and urged your own daughter
to move house too.

Ever ready to help,
she bought the last one in the row.
But it was a cold, cold winter.
Her journey to work, longer and colder than before.
And it was a bumper season for influenza.
She took ill, was hospitalized. The hospital gave her
drugs, which broke down her immune system.
She haemorrhaged. Pints of blood were transfused.
She asked for her much loved Brother, my Father,
saw him and died.

And you, Grandfather, what happened to you?
Too old to live in that bungalow alone,
you moved to live with your other daughter,
and, I guess, never saw your friend again,
let alone your generous daughter, the older twin,
who, 'though not knowing this at the time,
gave her life to your — absolutely understandable —
whim.   *Edited from notes, 2006*

Events and Encounters

Squirreling

I know you forget
where you've stored things away,
too.[7]

But,
what I'd like to know
is,
how you remember,
when you do.

December 2005

Events and Encounters

Parents and Children

When they die,
you realize
your parents
were not only father and mother,
but daughter and son too;
and always lived with the baggage,
which that experience
burdened
them
with.

October 2005

Events and Encounters

Always a Child

It may seem absurd
that a woman, sixty years old,
cries for her mamma.

But she's still a child,
inside;

as her mother was, too,
till she died.

Completed, June 2006

Events and Encounters

Politically Correct?

I am in a meeting.
Someone has been criticised,
for using the word, "hypocrisy".

He changes his vocabulary:
"Idealism, then", he says.

Goodness, how can he suggest
that hypocrisy and idealism
are <u>the same thing</u>?

But wait. . . .
<u>Does</u> he have a point?

Written c. 1982; edited, 2006

Events and Encounters

Unstained
From a would-be stain remover seeking in Shakespeare remedies for offence.

Pink is for courtesy,
Ophelia might have said.[8]

How you proved the point!

You never looked down, to see
how far the spilt red wine
your delicate pink incarnadined.[9]

Thank you!

Autumn 2005

Events and Encounters

Western Fung Shui Practitioner

Your crimson card
richly blazons your name;
and the gilt letters,
your proud profession.

But you dress yourself
in palest spring green —

a hopefully *modest* colour.

November 2005

Events and Encounters

The Value of Information

There, you've said it again. "I'm not well informed,
I'm afraid, but my husband is."

You're eighty-six; I'm fifty-seven.
As long as I remember, I've heard you say
the same thing.

                        Would there not have been time,
in fifty plus years, to acquire information for yourself,
if you really think it such a good thing?

Revised, June 2006

Events and Encounters

Permission

A child in hospital,
I heard the nurse
speak to the little boy
in the bed beside,
"You've wet the bed again", she scolded.
"Look at this little girl,"
pointing at me. "She didn't wet
<u>her</u> bed" and <u>she's</u> only three."

So the next night,
I did. And she couldn't say
<u>anything</u>.

Sixty years later, I
worked quite hard
on a small book catalogue;
and, after I finished, a kind friend said,
"I hope you didn't go mad
with all those books!"

And the next night,
I dreamt of putting book after book
in a database;
half awake, I input book after book, all night.

Strange, the things we're just
waiting permission to do!

Experienced, May 2006; completed, June 2006

Events and Encounters

Stiff Upper Lip[10]

It works like this. . .

Controlling your face
<u>not</u> to reflect the pain you feel
is no big deal, after a
life-time's restraint.

But it seems hardly fair,
when others don't care,
and doctors and physios
misdiagnose,

thinking that nothing is hurting.

In this scenario,
the stiffer your lip,
the longer your pain.

Better to learn to holler and cry
when nurses run by

abandoning childhood's training.

2006

Events and Encounters

Divine Discontent: an essay in Logic

Discontent comes easy, but divinity . . .?
Let's see. . . .
It hedges round a king,
as Shakespeare's Claudius claims:[11]

but it didn't save him from poison.
It didn't save Richard,
also asserting the "divine right of kings",
from prison or a violent death.[12]
Nor did it save Edward,
in Marlowe's play about another king,
from the three grimy smelly malcontents,
who laid a table on a featherbed above him,
and stamp-suffocated him to death.[13]
— Not easily got, or kept, then. Illusory.

Discontent, that grew to sudden sprouting
abundant harvest, rotting on the ground,
just by the eating of an apple
(sometimes aptly named Discovery);[14]
discontent, the spur that leads,
not only to ambition,[15]
but to pain, withdrawal, bitterness
— sad fruits indeed.

Remove the discontent!
Convert it to ambition!
But, without discontent,
in this particular equation,
divinity is lacking, too.
Which leaves the devil of ambition. . . . Oh!

1982; revised, Summer 2006

Events and Encounters

Parish Priest
For Mossèn Roc Pallarés Andorrà

We have watched you now for nineteen years;
serious, with your pleasant voice,
asking us questions and answering them,
always the same; asking and answering,
as if you knew we understood few words;
'though — I am sure — you deeply hoped
the Word[16] itself was something
all your congregation deeply knew.

We have watched you growing older,
still serious; and occasionally, in your hands,
saw the odd pleasure of a cigarette;
once or twice noted your brief chat
with doubtless useful parishioners.

Then, some years ago, we found a change.
A younger priest was there, in the church,
which, in your meekness,
probably, you never saw as yours
— except as it was ours — all of ours — too.

But still you sat or stood before us,
sharing the service,
assisting him,
who previously assisted you.

And still — no, more and more — your demeanour
teaches us what we should be: selfless, humble,
asserting not your own words,
but the Word made manifest through you.

Ordino, August 2006

Events and Encounters

Walking Stick

Walking along the path,
with the stick I gave my Father,
and which he used some years,
before he could not stride at all;
let alone pick a footing, through
such stony slate and dirt
as on these mountain paths;

I remember . . . he always took a stick
for country walks;
to indicate some distant view,
to scratch a grateful pig, or lean on,
pausing next to me, his only daughter,
arms full of summer bluebells,
or Easter primroses.

And, as I walk now,
leaning on this stick,
I try to send a message
through its point;

      to send him
pictures of these homely fields,
the horses' droppings (good for rhubarb),
the startled birds, red campion flowers,
white stitchwort; streams and pools. . . .

Such simple things may be omitted from heaven.

And he would enjoy them still, I know.

Ordino, August 2006

Events and Encounters

Warm Comfort

The dead are not like us,
because they are dead.[17]

Their thoughts are sublime, still,
spacious, focussed on immensity.

How can we cruelly beg them back,
with weeping, wailing, fixating,
passionate, heart-broken desiring and remorse?

Cut them loose from the strings of your heart! . . .
as God has loosed them
from the tugging strings
of their own days' interests,
duties, loves, desires,
struggles, pleasures and pains.

Cut them loose!

Let them rest and remain
above pleasure and pain!

Living requires us to do and feel,
believe in action, emotion, ambition,
loyalty, goals, success, desire.

So, we living think
we do the dead a favour,
when we share the village gossip
at their graves;[18]

show them respect,
feasting by stone tombs
at festivals,[19] calling their names,

Events and Encounters

urging them to eat and drink and mingle;
struggle to resume
an earthly perspective,
to please us.

We do not think we harm them,
when we descend into the underworld,
crudely spill some harmless creature's blood,
to force corporeality upon them;
simply for our information,
our own comfort,
to assist our purpose-making.[20]

Or when we visit Hades, dare the gods,
to beg them back,
exert our greatest charms,
woo them with our sweetest music,[21]
make them feel again
the enticements of the world,
where they can never live again.

We do not think it cruel, when we
place the letters of the alphabet
and a tumbler on a table,
and ask if anyone is there;[22]
when we urge our mangled soldiers
to remember, and then, let us know,
how much they suffered,
when they died.

As for the crude shrieks
and clanking chains,
which some of us imagine,
these reflect our need,
to be afraid;
not any need of theirs,
to cause us fear.

Events and Encounters

There are no restless, hungry ghosts of the dead;
just restless, hungry people, living in this world.

The dead will come back to us, but out of love.

They will wrestle themselves out
from the permanent peace
of their sublime sentience,
to visit us in dreams;
to comfort, assist, and renew
relationships, for our sakes.

No need to ask them.

When we need them, they will come.

They and we live
in the different spaces
of immensity and materiality.

The desire we living have
to reduce, breach and close
the separating space, and seize
the presence of the belovéd dead
is part of our living nature.

It is easy to think
we can bring the dead close
by blood, food, tears, festivals,
and gifts we easily find and offer,
and which we desire ourselves.

But, how hard it is
to reach — to seek to reach —
their unspoken silent sphere.

Events and Encounters

Yet, if we really love them,
more than we love our lives and living,
I think we would try . . . .

Henry Vaughan did it; lived it:[23]
"I saw eternity the other night,"[24] he wrote,
thinking of his twin and others who had gone
ahead of him, "into the world of light".[25]

And, when he died,
he had carved on his tomb
words which reveal his painful thoughts:

"Here lies one who longed to die,"[26] we read.

But . . .
such singleness of mood
is something we may not want,

at least not every day,

not in our living days.

Chester, United Kingdom, July 2006

Events and Encounters

Publication

Thoughts of the final casting off
concentrate the mind wonderfully,
I believe.

Certainly, the thought of publication does,
the mind of a poet,
I know.

1982; revised, Summer 2006

Events and Encounters

Cities of the Mind[27]

"How many days does my baby have to play?
Saturday, Sunday, Monday,
Tuesday, Wednesday, Thursday, Friday,
Saturday, Sunday, Monday."[28]

How many cities
can you hold in your mind?

Budleigh Salterton, Exmouth, Exeter, Conniton Raleigh,
Ottery Saint Mary, Taunton, Aberdare, Plymouth, Cardiff,
Tavistock, Axminster, London, Bournemouth,
Southbourne, Sidmouth, Teignmouth, Worcester, Malvern,
Birmingham, Paris, Avignon, Arles, Nimes, Les Saintes
Maries de la Mer, Valence, Frankfurt, Bishausen, Kassel,
Bristol, Clevedon, Hereford, Edinburgh, Manchester,
Lagos, Ibadan, Kano, Rome, Pompeii, Naples, Florence,
Venice, Milan, Badagri, Accra, New Delhi, Old Delhi,
Fatipur-sikri, Chandigarrh, Manila, Hong Kong, Macau,
New York, Boston, Princeton, Washington DC,
Charlottesville, New Orleans, Houston and Austin Texas,
Los Angeles, San Francisco, New Haven, Honolulu,
Geneva, Fort de France (Martinique), Melbourne,
Colombo, Kandy, Vancouver, Tokyo, Matsue (Japan),
Kyoto, Nara, that place in Italy, Bangkok, Auckland,
Wellington, King's Town & Spanish Town (Jamaica),
Mexico City, Phitsanulok, Sukhothai, Chengmai,
Singapore, Brussels, Totness, Tembelling Halt, Kuala
Lumpur, Penang, Helsinki, Aberdeen, Fraserburgh, Rathen,
Brisbane, Dubai, Andorra La Vella, La Massana, Arinsal,
Ordino, Seu d'Urgell, Beijing, Discovery Bay, Nanjing,
Suzhou, Barcelona, Munich, Shanghai, home. THIS IS A
WORK IN PROGRESS!

Updated, February 2007

Events and Encounters

Gift from an Astronaut[1]

"You have all my love."

"Thank you," she replies,
certainly
accepting the gift;

the gift confirming his previous gift;

the explicit, present, assurance,
that the gift of his love

stays with her,

now he is
overseas.

Revised, summer, 2006

---

[1] Hong Kong people have always traveled to make a living and many have lived overseas for a period to secure an overseas passport, for whatever reason. At a time when the number of families, with one family member living overseas, increased dramatically, the name, "astronaut" was given to the overseas partner, who flew back to Hong Kong, from time to time, to keep in touch with family and friends.

Events and Encounters

Transit Lounge. (Whiling away the time, waiting for a connecting flight.)

Waiting for hours together in an airport transit lounge,
perspectives change.

Humanity
is reduced
to these half human travelers,
stretched
out
on chairs, carpets and each other;
spirits dampened
by alienating suspension
between
one sphere
and the next.

Life itself is narrowed to these lanes of goods,
this processed food, these selected blandishments
from modern life.

But for me, this relaxed and happy thought arrives
and spreads its calm:

"I could walk with you for ever,
steadily and intimately
progressing,
through the shopping malls of life."

May 2006

Sightings
with
Mis-Communications

Sightings with Mis-Communications

Token

A single orchid[2]
blossoms
on the long stem,
extending
from
the slender strong branch of a
bauhinia tree:

delicate token of hope,
placed there by nature,
for us all to see,

if we will.

28 May 2004

---

[2] The Bauhinia is the flower, chosen to symbolize Hong Kong. The Bauhinia tree is sometimes called, "orchid tree".

Sightings with Mis-Communications

Doubt *or* "Are the laws of aerodynamics totally reliable?"

Look up!
Let your eyes penetrate
through the metal casing
of the newest model of plane!
See through, to
the rows of people,
sitting up there, in the sky!

Feel giddy fear
lest the laws of science
change
and they die!

28 May 2004; retitled, autumn 2006

Sightings with Mis-Communications

Too Much Reality

Within,
the packaged, neat and simple world
of the bus telescreen.

Outside,
the frightening uncontrolled variety
of life's reality.

28 May 2004

Sightings with Mis-Communications

In-fin-ity

In the kitchen,

waiting

for the drops of water
to drip off the slanted plate,

holding
the recently washed fish,

one has time

for thoughts

such as this:

"Everything is finite".

31 January 2006
(Pun by Verner Bickley)

Sightings with Mis-Communications

Cutting H[edge]

As we walked up the path
a boy played with a hedge cutter.

But on our return, no boy was seen;
just clippings of yew [you].

Completed, June 2006

Sightings with Mis-Communications

Shampoo Lady

Shampoo lady: "Excuse me?"
I open my eyes.
"Itchy?"²⁹
What does she mean?

Edited from notes, 2006

Ambiguous Advertising

"Escort service: no cover charge!"
— There is a charge if the escort is clotheless?³⁰

25 May 2004.

Ambiguous Praise: Flying High

An eagle climbs high,
but the sparrow on his back reaches higher.³¹

2001; retitled, autumn 2006

Difficult to Do

"Please use the stool available
to open your post office box."³²

October 2006

Sightings with Mis-Communications

Fashion Sense

She obviously likes that pink gingham hat.
—   And it is a nice hat.   —
The next step would be, to think
<u>how</u> to wear it,
not just carry it around
on the top of her head.

Completed, June 2006

Sightings with Mis-Communications

Curtains for Some

It's "Lo's Curtains" that faces
the mid-levels escalator, now,
replacing "Fetish Fashions" and its whips,
merry widows, leathers
and goodness knows which.

Strangely, in the middle
of fake medieval tapestries
and rich brocades,
Mickey Mouse cushions grin.

"It's curtains for some!"
Mickey chortles,
wondering when that naughty Minnie will come in.

Autumn, 2005

Sightings with Mis-Communications

Civil Contract, Hong Kong

The white pigeon,
landing on
curved spiked barbed railings,
painted government-blue,
in between Victoria Prison
and the old Central Police Station
on Old Bailey Street,
fluttering its wings and
angling its air-borne body,
as if making love,

symbolized what?

— What covenant, after what Noah's Flood?[33]
And between whom and whom?

What peace, what hope, what new beginning? —

Any of these? Or all?

Or none at all?

Autumn, 2005

Sightings with Mis-Communications

Balance

Helicopter landing near COSCO and IFC.[34]
Bird taking off from a building in Kowloon,
balancing each other.

I watch both from Hong Kong island.
My nearness to one
and my distance
from the other
makes each a similar size:
nature's bird and man's.

But in truth,
man's bird
dominates.

Anything else seems
illusion.

2004

Sightings with Mis-Communications

White Flags

They tell their message clearly:
white[35] strips of fabric,
lining hillside paths;
the freshly turned earth,
in horseshoe shape,
near to the previously paved
family tomb;
and the red strips,
tied to some living tree.

One being, gone.
And another life,
marked for destruction,
for all to see.

Was the human life slated for death,
equally clearly,
before the axe fell?

How sad for those,
who looked on!
How cruel of those,
who saw,
but did not grieve!

December 2005

Sightings with Mis-Communications

Fragile Symbols

Three bright triangular flags
fly bravely, pointing waterwards,
on the margin of the fishermen's island
that we pass, on the way to Tung Chung.[36]

What message do they have for us?
— Survival? Welcome? Veneration? Defiance? —

In quite different cultures,
fragile fabrics carry significances,
stronger than the
substance of our individual human lives;
and witness to them longer, too.

Memory calls to mind
heraldic hangings, threadbare
with their ghosts of messages,
in distant, dim English cathedrals,
where instants are lengthened, perpetuated.

The media used are similar;
but the messages, probably, are different.

Each, paradoxically,
communicates only to those,
who know the message already.

Why have the symbols then?
Are we so bad at remembering?

3 November 2005

Sightings with Mis-Communications

Battle Sight

On a new burial on the hillside above Pak Mong, a fishing village, passed on the road between Discovery Bay and Tung Chung, Lantau Island, New Territories, Hong Kong.

The fallen poles and
bedraggled
strips of white
still lie
where you lie:

useless discarded spears
in the fight for life.

December 2005

Sightings with Mis-Communications

Asphalt Flower

When I first saw you,
your wings
were still upright;
their fluttering
conceivably
your remaining
attempt
to stay
balanced
on the huge grey
asphalt flower
with the dust-black pollen,
where you'd landed.

Waiting for the lights to change,
I saw the wheels avoid you,
then hit you, turn you, crush you,
flatten your wings,
toss and re-crush you.

By the time I crossed the road,
you were not there
at all.

June 2004

Sightings with Mis-Communications

Christmas Bear [-hug]

Lines on the figure of a bear, standing at the side of the pavement along Nathan Road, Kowloon, Hong Kong, seen November 2004 (still in place, 2006). The quoted words in the poem are written on the bear.

"Love" on your belly,
"Happiness" and "Harmony"
under your armpits,
you hold up your arms
in an unambiguously
joyous gesture,
seeking to embrace us all;
offering a Christmas bear-hug to the world.

December 2004

Sightings with Mis-Communications

Leaves:[37] Street Sweeper and Teacher Compared

If there were no trees,
there would be
no leaves,
no work
for you to do.

If there were no students
there would be
no paper assignments,
no salary,
for me.

Edited from notes, summer and autumn, 2006

Sightings with Mis-Communications

Differences

What different concerns, each of us has!
The roadman urgently waves his mate
to pack away traffic cones and clear the lane.
Four yards away, on the green, road-side slope,
a small, yellow butterfly flutters and chooses
and lands on a particular flower.

Hugely different too, are the thoughts,
directing each of our minds,
and each of our separate actions too.

No wonder we can't always find
a matching mood,
even in those we know best.

June 2004

Sightings with Mis-Communications

Mediterranean Reaction

Every now and then,
I get a glimpse
of a mediterranean reaction: —

to the sea,
the casuarina trees,
the interminably slow-
growing sea-shore shrubs,
which, only after fifteen years, outgrow
their air of fasting bonsai;[38]
the velvet-needled, caterpillar-thick fern,
like branches of Lake Geneva pines;
the white-plastered three-storeyed villas
spreading backwards from the sea.

And I wonder if <u>this</u>
is the Hong Kong people leave,
claiming it has disappeared?

Is it only we, of later date,
who see these glimpses,
sniff the elusive scent of Europe?

And the reason? — Because
<u>our</u> more recent Europe,
with its high-rise flats, dust, and road repairs,
resembles, now, what
old-timers see
as the Asian horror
of modernising Hong Kong?

Written c. 1982; edited, summer, 2006

Sightings with Mis-Communications

First Impressions

From airport to capital,
Asian countries lead you on and in,
over wonderful roads.

Singapore drips bougainvillea.
Phuket formerly bounced you steamily
past rubber plantations, rice fields,
and shy beauties at work in the sun.
And Kuala Lumpur (KL to some)
shelters us with tall trees.

Hong Kong juxtaposes
wild country and cultivated verge,
both lying endlessly open,
unprotected and exposed,
under live power lines, clearly visible.
Looking up, we see waterworks,
and the steps for reaching them.

Let's hope some trees
will grow quickly
and hide
the sewage plant,
nakedly seen, also alongside.

2004

Sightings with Mis-Communications

Disappearing Harbour

I thought Harry Ricketts'[39] picture
of the fluid, coloured fish
   — swimming in the dark
Hong Kong harbour, at nights,
just right;
provocative, deep —
brought to us
by the night and the lights
of the buildings, which were shorter then,
in the seventies.

But you were right too,
when you observed
that this no longer attracts.
People now admire the hard laser beams,
slicing across the harbour:[40] . . .
hard cutting thoughts
replacing softer ways.

Let's do the same!
Then — at nights, at least — raising
our eyes,
we will not notice,
when the day comes,
when the harbour has

        entirely gone.

October 2005

Sightings with Mis-Communications

Coffin Play[41]

On a coffin-shaped slab
of concrete seating,
the old man and his wife sat,
relaxing, carefree.

In front and below them,
a few feet away,
the flat squares of a
piazza-size
musical fountain
gleamed.

The old man lent back on his arms,
stretched out his toes and wriggled them,
shaking off rainbow water-drops.

Half turned towards him,
his wife sat behind,
easily exercising
her more limber shoulders.

Self-absorbed,
they seem not to see
the few children
playing near.

— Freeze it in time! —

this happy and calm
emblem of married life:

more intimate,
more warmly accessible
than the prone knight and lady,
carved, dead, on their tomb,

Sightings with Mis-Communications

hand holding stone-carved hand,
flat on their backs, gazing skyward,
whom Larkin[42] describes with such
suitably complex emotion and thought.

June 2004

Rowboat

Rowboats and adults' coffins
are similarly shaped:

with the broad shoulders at the boat's beam,
and the narrower feet at the bow;

each built to go
through the sunset, facing a distant escape . . .

Revised, Summer 2006

Sightings with Mis-Communications

Spectacles

For a socially committed poet, whose recent collection of poems was printed in very small type-face.[43]

You see the ills of the world
quite clearly,
wishing that others would do the same.

But you wear glasses.

To train us to see as you do,
you publish words,
too small for us
to read
without glasses,
too.

Noted 2004; completed, 27 January 2006

Sightings with Mis-Communications

Images

In Nigeria, in the sixties,
local women and men enjoyed Indian films,
set in Europe's capitals and landscapes;
oohing and aahing at the Trevi Fountain,[44]
Versailles,[45] the Queen of England's castles;
and took quite in their stride—
as entirely unremarkable—
helicopters, assembled in five minutes
from a fleeing car; and other incidents
that appeared to me more fancifully then,
than they do now.

Now, in the early two thousands,
I, similarly, watch—for the setting—cable news:
to see, for example, Nigeria itself, (where Miss World[46]
 two-oh-oh-two was scheduled to take place);
Iraq (where they played the grim game
of weapons' inspection, and its ruler, Saddam Hussein,
gave a bland, confident greeting to his realm,
denying they had any);
Indonesia (where people are rioting),
Australia (with its bush fires);
Venezuela (where people are also rioting);
West Spain (where oil is polluting the shore);
Italy (where Fiat workers are protesting);
Croatia (where a recent election has failed);

and view, as comparatively mundane,
the less scenic and more abstract
threats—of pollution and eventual, total, war.

Edited from pre "9/11" notes, 2006

Sightings with Mis-Communications

Sweet Provider

Two years ago, or so,
every-one started putting out
glass bowls of sweets and chocs,
to sweeten encounters
that might be disturbing, time wasting,
or otherwise irritate:—
departments at universities,
immigration officials,
banks, even shopping centres.

New arrivals must wonder
about it. Perhaps they consider
that this is the accepted way
of getting a sweet to munch on.

Certainly, the woman who
scooped up three in her palm,
as she rushed on her way
through IFC2,[47]
anxious perhaps to gamble
millions away in Macau,
completely ignoring
the young receptionist lady—
sitting demure and patient as always
in the curve of the corridor,
ready to direct lost folks on their way—
was not, to my way of thinking,
playing the expected game.

Autumn, 2005

Sightings with Mis-Communications

Thoughtfulness

The paper offerings
for the souls of the dead[48]
thoughtfully include
a calculator, mobile phone and watch.

A calculator can count the cost of their own funeral.
A mobile phone can contact friends wherever they are
(if there is satellite cover).

But does one need a measurement for time,
when time has stopped
completely;
when the sands of life
have finally run out?

Perhaps
those surviving
need
to think on different lines?

Perhaps they are really
not
very thoughtful,
after all?

4 November 2005

Sightings with Mis-Communications

"City Golf Club"

The white pom-pom chrysanthemums
of last night's tee-off
lie in their hundreds on the fake greens.

On the verges, water sprinklers play.
Maybe the golf-balls will burst into flower;
the plastic grass come to life,
and the city gents who go there
blossom into world-class talents,
some distant day?

October 2006

Sightings with Mis-Communications

Her Choice

She was a big woman, tall and stately,
and she always wore white:[49]
white pleated silk skirt, down to her ankles;
white silk stockings;
white leather shoes, with moderately high heels, straps and
    buttons;
a white loose blouse, with long sleeves, flounces, and frills;
and a big white hat, with a half veil, topped by a big,
stuffed, white bird.
Her face was white too, painted with thick powder,
white as flour. She carried a soft silk handbag;
and, in her other hand,
a white parasol in the Edwardian[50] fashion.

We saw her on Sunday afternoons, sometimes;
young girls going to Sunday school.
We stared and looked, as she
measured the city pavement
slowly, undisturbed.
"She lives in such and such a home",
one of us would say. "But she's alright. She can come out,
whenever she wants. She was jilted at the
altar, ever so long ago, years and years ago,
and this is what she wore, as she
waited for him, then."
Another story was, that her sweetheart
died in the war — the Great War
(nineteen fourteen eighteen), that would be.

But always, it was a man,
whom we deemed to be the cause
of her choice for her life.

Sightings with Mis-Communications

For, however deeply buried
that choice was, it <u>was</u> a
choice, was it not?

Some of us knew her name,
and it seemed strange to me,
that this detached presence had any-
thing so personal as a name; that one of us
could have such intimate knowledge
of a personage so august.[51]

Miss What-was-your-name,
what was in your mind,
as you progressed
down the empty Sunday streets,
turning neither right nor left,
always facing straight ahead,
with imperturbable tread?

Stripped of the present,
were they more familiar then?
Did your eye acknowledge only older buildings,
present since your youth?
  — The Star Hotel, the Angel, and the Crown,[52]
where you may have taken "refreshment";[53]
Pump Street Methodist Church,
which would have frowned if you did;
Grey Friars[54] and the Cathedral (once a monastery church),
institutions, where surplus males (accumulated after years
of peace, when man-made selfish folly and his clever new
inventions had not yet wiped out
millions of young men,
and by the same slaughter,
stripped their wives and the young girls growing up
of companionship, love, children and previously expected
    purpose):

Sightings with Mis-Communications

White Friars and the Cathedral, then, where surplus males,
in former times,
found a pattern and a style of life,
by which to endure the years—
things you found for yourself,
and which also had, in their own way,
dignity, remarkability,
beauty, and a kind of fulfillment;
the Shambles[55] and the Hop Market,[56]
where the grosser needs of food and drink
were copiously—and partly brutally—available;
the Friends' Meeting House,[57] where
your silence would have been
nothing unusual; though its message,
some might have thought too violent
a painful protest;
the Commandery, headquarters, for a time,
in England's bloody civil war;
when puritan—later Protector—Cromwell
and always cavalier King Charles fought
for the life-style they and their people preferred,[58]
as President Mr George born-again-christian Bush
and the Al Quaeda group each do today;
Foregate Street railway bridge, bearing
the three black pears, which Worcester—loyal city,
"civis fidelis"[59]—gave to Elizabeth the First,
hundreds of years ago,
when her royal Progress[60] took her there from London:

—an earlier spinster; who found that single state,
with her careful guidance of her English nation State,
two callings, worthy of her passionate embrace.
As for you, late Edwardian dame,
were you there to see,
or, like the Queen, to be seen?

Sightings with Mis-Communications

Were you refreshing the past,
re-printing old city sights on your mind?
In imagination,
were you walking with your beau,
strolling slowly, enjoying love's young dream,
walking for the sake of it, with no destination
but the heart's fulfillment, which never came?

Or, in your mind's eye, did you see
him, waiting for you,
at the end of this long, familiar street?

Were you consciously showing,
with your calm advance,
and focused, undeflected confidence,
his loyal love, your faithful fancy?—
conveying also, but with less intention,
the profound depths, where you had buried—
and for years kept buried—your sharp,
sad knowledge of the cynical way, the world had taken,
destroying the dreams of your long-past,
decades-old, youth?

Seen 1950s; written 2006

Sightings with Mis-Communications

Aperçus:[61] Encountered on a Walk round the Peak

Is it a leaf falling, soundless, brown,
or a butterfly, silently visiting
sites, where nectar was found
last summer?

What a scurry you make
with that long blue tail of yours
whacking the boughs,
cock-pheasant.

Morning-glory,[62]
I did not know
you curled up for the night;
feeling shy,
regretting the recurring
loss of the brighter sky,
and your Father, the sun.

It is difficult to find
the paths we trod last year.
Was it there?
Was it here?

Screechily singing cricket,[63]
rasping like a saw,
or a door that creaks,
are you so small
that you make a big noise
out of fear?

Japanese maple,
with leaves like paper,
wilfully playing games with the wind,

Sightings with Mis-Communications

I guess you know
no-one can fine you,
for the litter you make,
just like an under-age child!

Nobody steals
those brooms and those baskets,
trustfully left for tomorrow´s work.
—I wonder why?—
Do they fear, the penalty may be
to sweep the Peak for ever?

Jagged epiphyte,[64]
comfortably sitting
in that arched bole,
cushioned smoothly
by round penny-wort;[65]
you chose the very place,
where I would sit, if I were you.

Wildly waggling leaves,
why do you, alone,
move eccentrically?
No animal is digging at your roots,
as I can see.
Do you wish to pull up from the soil,
and so, wildly try, try . . .
until, by your dancing, you die?

Rook, you sound like a tom-cat[66]
calling a mate. Auw Auw.
And now ererh ererh,
like a cat that has found one.
Black cap, "pink", "pink",
perky as a pirate,
your grey breast, stained by blood,

Sightings with Mis-Communications

why do you fly jerkily away,
when you see that I watch you?

Was I standing so still,
that you thought me a tree
and flew into me,
black butterfly, studded with white?

The mist has come down.
The hills' outlines glow
with the sinking sun.

Time to go home.

Leaves, how can you be
so many shapes and sizes?
Can you still know you are all
close members of one family?

Squirrel, you sat
quite calmly grooming,
until the thump of the runners
was really quite near.
Then you moved smoothly
upward to the tree-tops.
You may be deaf,
but you know that we aren't blind.

Bull-frog, shouting for love in an echoing drain . . .
The largest group here, on this hill,
seems to be birds:
tramping through the leaves,
as loud as people do.

Sightings with Mis-Communications

The waterfall has shrunk.
It sounds like a tap left on,
filling a plastic bucket.

Has a human uprooted you, tree,
that you lie, untidily cumbering the path?
And you in bud too! Ah, cruel!

White flowers! I have finally found
who perfumes the air. It is you!

The islands seem like clouds;
the clouds, like islands.
Twilight magically
twists
how we see
the view.

Trees, be more careful.
If your roots
break up the tarmac
any more,
you will be cut down.

A part of man
partly lives here, too.

Revised, Summer 2006

Sightings with Mis-Communications

What Bird Flew?

You stand there, exotic even among the exotic:

 ... 'though how one can find exotic
this remote village,
these broken-down paint-peeling-from rafts,
and these few outboard motors,
is — when you think about it — surprising.

I know your profile, but not your name.
— I must look it up in a book of Birds,
under "Winter Visitors".[67] —

You flew in, when? Do you know about
"bird 'flu"? Are you poised there,
outside the village, alone,

unsure of your welcome,

or,

afraid that you'll catch it from us?

Observed in Hong Kong,
25 January;
written 26 January 2006

Sightings with Mis-Communications

The Watcher Watched

An apparently perfectly normal man
held out his arms stiffly like
the wings of a plane,
revolved in a small half-circle,
and went back the way he came.

I stood and watched him
to see if anything else eccentric
would follow, but nothing did.

As I stopped my own eccentric, still, stance,
moved out from the middle of the passageway,
positioned myself to cross the road,
I saw two hard-hatted workers,
sitting on a low wall, resting.
One — all animated — was miming
the first eccentric's airplane movements.
I think he glanced in my direction too,
telling his mate, "That's what
she was watching too, you know"!

Observed May/June 2006; completed, 29 June 2006

Sightings with Mis-Communications

Young Master

I've given up
peering into
very grand cars
with special number plates,
to see if I know
who's inside.

— I rarely do. —

But today, I forgot about that.

— Beige. Large.
— Bentley? . . . Mercedes?[68] — I didn't know.

And I peered to look in.

Inside, back right in the
master's seat,
behind the driver

sat a small boy, feet
sticking out, unable to touch the floor,
munching sweets
out of a coloured, paper-covered tube.

I didn't know him either! Do you?

October 2005

Sightings with Mis-Communications

Is there Heartbreak in Heaven?

The small boy looked hopefully
between the tall lolloping Englishman, his father,
and his plump young mother,
neatly dressed in white trousers and shirt;
hoping that at least one of them would share
one of their two bottles of water with him.

Of course, one marries who is there,
not thinking of the girl left at home next door,
always hoping that the next day will bring
his long-awaited letter. A century ago
the man did return—to Scotland, say[69]—
leaving his home away from home
in the strange distant land that had,
partly, become his, because of her.

Men must adapt and women . . .
must accommodate,[70]
to what their man decides to do.

But God plays his part too.

Sometimes men move further off,
to the other side of time.

Once there, do their hearts bleed
when they see the new arrangements
their woman makes, down here below?

Is their heartbreak in heaven, too?

Observed, June 2006; completed, 29 June 2006

Sightings with Mis-Communications

Creating Words

The cold winds of Easter—
unexpected as the crucifixion was
to the carpenter's son,
who was born
two thousand years ago—

blow our thoughts to the colder
home which we came from
and the faithful parents
whom we had,

quietly resisting
differences of faith,

while united
in duty,
good citizenship.

Easter comes as the
heritage gift,
man has created
for comfort;

a bed of intertwined thoughts,
allowing us to picture the
resurrection of those
we know;

not their total elimination.

Sightings with Mis-Communications

The sponge of vinegar, which the Roman soldier
offered Christ on the cross,[71]
prevents the expunging of lives
and the good all lives have
been, done, and thought.

The sweet struggling mimosa opening in
the astonishing cold
is a symbol that faith
can
triumph.
. . .
And words can create faith.

Easter 2006

Sightings with Mis-Communications

Roman Stones[72]
"H. F. C. Heres Faciendum Curavit"
("*The heir arranged the making of this stone*")

Who would have thought, in this small,
inelegant, and crowded space, funded
by a lord's beneficence and public gaming funds,[73]
that one would find such vivid Roman
presences? Centurions[74] and their wives from
AD hundreds one to three. Goddess Minerva
with her owl and shield, helmet and spear.
Twin slave boys, dead aged ten or twelve. And
the to-us-touching words (to Romans, maybe,
merely a convention-keeping phrase):
"To the spirit of the departed, Julia.
She lived sixty years. Her heir had this made."

The symbols of the sea, by which
they signified the journey spirits made
to the Blessed Isles—sea shells, dolphins. . . .

The doves pecking at grapes . . .

The smiling faces of the dead as they recline,
raising in one hand their final, eternal glass of wine.

Mother goddess, Cybele, with her partner Attis,
and their mysterious rites, promising life after death:
an offer which few Roman boys took up.—
Self-castration here—
which the cult presented
as a necessary measure,
for securing the hereafter —
most did not fancy much.—

Sightings with Mis-Communications

"Marcus Aurelius Nepos, centurion of the Twentieth Legion.
His most dutiful wife had this made. He lived fifty years."
The carving shows us Marcus, and next to him, his wife,
formed on a smaller scale,
who inexplicably holds up her skirt, quite high.
What did she mean?

Whatever people thought about her gesture then,
we later folk can't help but take the view
that this immodesty (as we see it, now)
likely explains why her death is not recorded here at all!

As for Sextus Similius from Brescia, in the Italian North,
two lions flank his stone portrait, recording
a sudden and quite unexpected end.

—Such deep emotion these remnants of past Roman lives evoke,
with their odd strange similarity to ourselves!—

"Daddy," a small visiting boy brightly says,
"When you see this, it takes you back!"

Proud of his son, his father
seeks to elaborate on this clear perception.
But the small boy had said it all.
It takes you back!

Chester, UK, Summer 2006

From a Novel in Progress

From a Novel, in Progress

Illusions
(from a novel, in progress)

What furtive life you have,
you secret man,
who was her husband;

sitting there
primly self-contained,
while others
are matey matey
at the bar.

By your tense precision,
can you still succeed—
twice divorced as you've been—
in fooling others—
as you did her—
that the stories
of young single girls
and yourself
are quite absurd?

More important,
do you succeed,
as it seems you wish,
in deceiving
yourself?

Revised, Summer 2006

From a Novel, in Progress

Deserts
(from a novel, in progress)

If she is a thing to be deserved,
then surely you deserve her.
For you fructify each other, loves.

The she you hold
is what she is with you.

And as she walks the world—you absent—
modified by you, she is;
and growing
by
continuing debate
with what you say and are.

You too, she hopes.

Revised, Summer 2006

From a Novel, in Progress

Butterfly
Dramatic Monologue
(from a novel, in progress: the female protagonist speaks)

"How long ago was it
that you took me
to a Gallery in Washington?
I can't remember its name. I should,
but I can't.
I've never been good with names. I could look it up.
But you know where I mean.
You made me walk fast along hard pavements
to get there;

"your hands clasped behind your back
(I'm sure not copying Philip,[75]
as his son, Charles,[76] does)
making your head poke forwards with its spade beard,
talking in your nice accent that sounds to me
warm and countrified, as in Cornwall or Somerset,[77]
but to an American, I'm sure, has far <u>other</u> connotations . . .
what, I've never found anyone to ask, who might
answer, knowing you and knowing America too.

"'I'll take you to the Whistler Room,'[78] you say.

"'See, in every picture there's a butterfly.
He made it as it were his signature.
And there's his Woman in White.
It caused a great scandal in London.'[79]
"—Something to do with Ruskin[80] and a penny costs in
　　court.
Or was it a ha'penny or a shilling?[81]
—a small amount in any case;
but enough to cause shame, the court costs to cause penury;

From a Novel, in Progress

and all to cause
Whistler's departure from England, for a while;
everyone knowing, a leading critic had said he was a cheat,
imposing on the English public
by flinging a paint-pot in its face,
or something like that.

"And then, years later,
after time, served[82] with the man I later married,
I was with you again in Washington,
in another gallery;[83]
up steps across a green open space,
with bus stops and untidy people lounging there.
Again, I've forgotten its name.

"Some man, who'd made money in Russia, selling arms
—or was it grain—
after the war.
And he was able—was it because he was clever,
or they were grateful?—
to collect vast treasures of the art-loving
(or maybe, merely art-collecting) Czars.

"And we walked around.

"And I was brilliant. I was clever and witty,
incisive and sharp. I saw things in the pictures, I've
never seen in pictures before. You potentiated me.

"But then my husband begged me back.

"I went.
"Later, I discovered he'd been faithless for years,
spending private time with a girl, whom I still call whore,
even before our marriage.

From a Novel, in Progress

"I divorced him.

"But you were in a pique. You refused to come
to visit me in England.

"Did you feel your artistry,
your creation of a new myself,
had been unappreciated by its only public, me?

"Oh you were wrong!

"But Pinocchio's 'Papa' —Guiseppe—
found
even his hand-made puppet danced away.[84]

"And George du Maurier was wrong[85] to think
talented Trilby could not live,
beyond her hypnotist, Svengali's, death.

"This I know. A soul-made influence
cannot bind the soul it frees
and makes to soar.
It has to let it go,
and risk
the chance
that the pleasure of its free return
may never come.

"Or was it that my husband's threats to you,
of suing you
for damages,
struck a loud bell that caused alarm?

"—Although absurd.—

From a Novel, in Progress

"The next time
I am in Washington,
I shall be with another man.

"You will be thinking
the butterfly[86]
should be my signature too!

"After what new experiences,
will I find myself again with you
in a gallery in Washington,

"if ever?"

1980's; edited, 2006

From a Novel, in Progress

Labels
(from a novel, in progress)

In the country suburbs,
in the autumn colours and damp grey,
which glowed with burnished light;
the leaves
proclaiming
their vivid life,
in the act of death;

the man and woman looked for a place
to stop and eat.

Its subdued air
made him feel
that the large place they found
was in private hands.

Its Diners Club[87] sign meant
she could not agree.

Are these the lessons she should learn?

That labels lie,
appearances sometimes deceive,

but he (and not she)
knows what's what?

—I don't think he would mind!

Revised, Summer 2006

From a Novel, in Progress

She would have been here
(from a novel, in progress)

Had she met you here, among blue calls of jays,
the soft crackling of dropping excrement,
seeping from caterpillars,
concealed overhead,
in green-sunned leaves;

had she met you here,
been familiar already
with customs and ways,

like you; cossetted habitually
by the comfort of kind friends;

there would have been less fear
that she would be banished from you,
or you from her.

There would have been
more room
for joy in talk, for being-with.

There would have been
no need
for questions of whether, or if;
or, should she—or you—go, or stay;

For already,
you both would have been here.

Revised, Summer 2006

From a Novel, in Progress

Favour
(from a novel, in progress)

She has wrapped you
with so many folds of favour,
enfolded you
in her heart's innermost embrace;
and now, perhaps,
the necessary thing
may be
to remove her love from you,
to separate your flesh from hers,

so that, when separation comes,
the wounds already may be cauterised;
the blood clots formed;
the wounds not new, tho' newly rubbed with salt.

How can she do it?
She, who eagerly saw all, approvable;
all, all beloved.
How can she
teach herself to see
an opposite thing;
to cease to love
the one her soul approves?

Revised, Summer 2006

From a Novel, in Progress

Cold Dawning
(from a novel, in progress)

The grey, cold, moonless, sunless dawn
is creeping over their cold feet;
their hearts, grown cold
from talking about why
"they" rejected "them". A bright star
—the brightest—
has fallen from their sky.

Revised, Summer 2006

From a Novel, in Progress

Shelter, Foetus
(from a novel, in progress)

Like an aborted foetus,
a grey and detached blood bone flesh ball
of grey dead possible life, love, hope,

the thought of you is floating away,

distantly floating.

Is it no more than this?

—this unattractive lump of matter,

which she allows to detach itself from her
and float, float away?

—The calm and horror of letting it go!—

The umbilical cord,
defying the laws of gravity, lies horizontal
in the air, its long length towards her.

Is it possible she still can act to save?

—reach out her hand, grasp, pull (gently, pull,
do not harm or hurt, further)
and by complicated micro-surgery of love, patience,
self-abnegation, pushing down all "I want" thoughts
and thinking "what you want,
"what will help you grow back into me",
re-grow the pulsing link of love and nutrience?

From a Novel, in Progress

Then ultimately, the healthy life of a plump
and kicking child can grow outside her care;
your linked selves part walk,
independent of your separate lives,

strengthening as you grow old,

until at last
it gives you shelter in its spacious boughs.

Revised, Summer 2006

From a Novel, in Progress

Brief Bloom
(from a novel, in progress: first, the female protagonist speaks)

"Is life then to be
un-immanent with thee?
the striking hour to say,
not, 'Day is passing day,
soon will come the night,
and my bright love of loves
pass through the door
for evermore, each day.'

"But, 'Day is passing day,
and your dear love must lay
his head somewhere at night,
but not by yours.'"

The pregnant moon
swells,
and delivers,
each lunar season,
her sharp sliver[88] son.
But you have given a reason,
why her season
for such boastfulness
will never come
by you, and hence
will never come.

The trees' juices annually renew
their vivid green,
and every year their beauty seen, as ever, fair.

From a Novel, in Progress

Her fallow contours sag;
her colours fade;
the spurting life
hesitates,

and her soul
—the phoenix
which must soar
from ashes of fond flesh[89]—
plucks courage
hardlier, each year
she waits for you,
knowing you will not come.

Her waiting is her sacrifice,
her fragrant blossom
of devotion;
exotic bloom among
the ruthless growths,
snatching any flesh
to suck and set up house.

Self-gardener to her flower,
she tends and patients it,
plucks out encroaching growths,
rings it fairily
with gardener's poison,
isolates its fruit.

And, after many years,
at night,
for one hour only,
it will bloom;
its beauty,
fiercely soft
and lonely.

From a Novel, in Progress

You will not pluck her.
You will not touch her.
But may the fragrance reach you then!

Ah, be there!
Be there,
to see!

Revised, Summer 2006

From a Novel, in Progress

The Visit
(from a novel, in progress)

And this is your house in the woods,
where small deer tread the fallen leaves,
delicately tentative;
crossing from another place to somewhere else . . .
on their way . . .
passing through . . . not calling by; aware
that this is your house in the woods;

but feeling no warmth for you,
having no knowledge of you
as any kin of theirs;
alert to hurry and run,
to scamper and panic,
once they know you are near.

How different she,
coming from another place and going
back there, indeed;
but, centred here, staying here at peace
however far she goes.

And this because of you;
her being informed with peace
because of you,
opening still and quiet
when your hand reaches out
to touch her.

Inconceivable
to startle, remove herself in spirit, scamper away,
protecting her existence
from the consequences of yours.

From a Novel, in Progress

And you—somewhat akin to your
delicate steppers-by—
how will you act?

If she comes too near,
if you discover suddenly
how near she is,
will it startle you
from the calm
of your new creation
of each other and yourselves,

rush you from your own home
into the wildness of cold out there;

sending her back somewhere else,

where she will, only occasionally,
see the delicate marks in the snow:
proof that there was a you, that
the two of you were once there?

But when the snow melts,
they will be gone too.

Revised, Summer 2006

Communicating Poems

Based on a Talk given at a Hong Kong Baptist University Department of English Language and Literature Staff Seminar on Monday, 24 April 2006. Expanded and revised.

Introduction
I am going to consider the practicalities of addressing both local and global audiences in a single edition of poetry, referring to my first two poetry collections, *Moving House and other Poems from Hong Kong* and *For the Record and Other Poems of Hong Kong*.

I believe that the topic will be of interest to you, as readers of literature at least, some of you as teachers of literature and/or literary critics, and others still as creative writers and editors as well.

We are all familiar with literary editing – whether of poetry books or other texts – which provides some biographical information about the writer or writers of the work(s), some commentary on the origin and background to the work(s) and some explanation of local references and background, as well as of "difficult" or specialized words. Some editions may provide comments on literary technique and the past publishing history and reception of a work.

In the case of a new work, or a work issued during the writer's lifetime, all this information may or may not have been provided by the author(s) or alternatively researched by the editor(s). (Most likely, even when the information has been contributed by the author, this is not acknowledged.) In the case of a work issued <u>after</u> the writer's lifetime, all the information must, of course, necessarily be researched and/or compiled during the editorial process.

In all cases, however, editorial elements, such as those I have listed, together with the overall presentation of the text, are carefully considered from the point of view of the targeted readership as well as from a cost and/or marketing perspective. Typically, texts published with the general reader in mind have fewer notes than those for school or university use, or for those bearing in mind readers of English as a second language.

The global spread of English as a language of international communication, combined with increasingly efficient international distribution of texts on first publication and before they have had time either to mature into classics or disappear from long-term consideration, means that the readers who can access newly published texts are so very diverse that it may be impossible to provide adequate commentary to accommodate the legitimate expectations of all. In these circumstances, is it valid to make the attempt to explain? Or should the text be presented naked of commentary, to sink or swim according to the experience, information and linguistic sophistication of the multitude of readers whom it may encounter? Is it purely a costing and marketing decision? Or should it be a matter of concern to writers themselves? Should they themselves offer the necessary editorializing, if they can? Failing this, should they seek to purge their writing of any content other than what they may suppose is part of our global culture? Would such an attempt succeed only in rendering their work less valuable, rich and interesting?

I remember an interesting scene in Han Suyin's novel, set in Hong Kong, *A Many-Splendored Thing*, published in the USA in c. 1952, where the artist friend of the heroine says, given that, "everyone can read these days", graphic art is a safer means of expression than writing, because no-one knows what a graphic artist actually means.

Does the fact that, in this first decade of the twenty-first century, verbal communication can be disseminated, better than ever before, mean that the content of what can be communicated needs to be, or perhaps actually has been, reduced? And is that reduction proportional to the increased spread of what is communicated?

My topic is taken from the perspective of publishing in Hong Kong; but could be applied to publishing based in any other locality. I will consider very briefly seven points: inter-textuality, cultural references, local references, translation, simplicity of diction and expression, careful editing for the sake of clarity and communicability, and finally, graphic means of underlining or conveying at least part of the meaning of the poem.

I was impressed when, at a recent Hong Kong Baptist University English Department Seminar, Xu Xi made the point that writers "take in" from their surroundings and then give it back in artistic expression. This is, of course, true. But, given that it is true, it may be unlikely that individual readers have experienced, and "taken in" from their surroundings, everything that the writer they are reading has "taken in". In this case, to what extent can writers expect or rely on the reader to infer meaning from the text itself? To what extent do writers need to explain their meaning themselves, by including their own annotations, not waiting for any editor or literary critic to do this job in many years time, if at all?

Inter-textuality

The first topic I will consider is inter-textuality, because the question of whether or not to annotate inter-textuality seems to be a relatively clear-cut topic.

I offer first what *I* consider a charming example. In the academic year, 2003-2004, when still a member of Faculty in the English Department at Hong Kong Baptist University, I taught Laurie Lee's *Cider With Rosie* in some detail, compiling and handing out copious notes. In her response to an assignment I gave to the class, a student wrote as follows. "We miss the past because we came from there. As we get older, we have more memories and are

Communicating Poems

even more reluctant to change".[90] These clear concepts impressed me and I wrote this poem in response, quoting her first sentence.

Past Present
(*Moving House* (MH), 2005, p. 39)

We miss the past because we came from there:
— people and scenes and places, and ways of doing things: —

old women, mumping their lips in the sun;
old men, eating their breakfast,
outside the Museum of Heritage,
at Shatin;
university students,
cherishing school friends,
from primary and secondary days.

And I, do I miss the past, too?

Not yet, not yet.

I embrace the present,
in embracing you.

But I
surely know
the past is where we also come from;
and where we're going, too.

Only I myself and the student in question knew the sequence of influences that led to this poem. Unless I had told the student, even she could only have guessed that there were any specific influences at all. I am quite sure that I was right in including a note, explaining this (MH, p.

125, n. 6). The reference to the student's work, however, is in the nature of an acknowledgement of a source, rather than a necessary explanation of meaning to readers; and so is the reference to the primary source of influence, Laurie Lee's work.

However, in other cases, the explanation of intertextuality in my two collections aims to supply a different type of information, which readers not only might not possess, but which is necessary if readers are to begin to grasp what I had in mind.

First, some examples from *Moving House and Other Poems from Hong Kong* (MH). There are references to Lewis Carroll's *Alice in Wonderland* in "Progressive Movement" (MH, p. 37); to Virgil's *Æneid* in "Christmas Letters from Afar" (MH, p. 40); and George Elliot's *Middlemarch* in "Marriage" (MH, p. 44).

Examples in my earlier collection, *For the Record and other Poems of Hong Kong* (FTR), are: references to Thomas Carlyle's "Sartor Resartus" in my poem by the same name (FTR, p. 29); the anonymous ballad, "Sir Patrick Spens" and St Matthew's Gospel in the Holy Bible, both in "Newsworthy" (FTR, p. 38); and also to Alfred Lord Tennyson's "The Death of Arthur" in "Approaching Tai Po Highway, Speeding Home" (FTR, p. 69).

I say "begin to grasp", rather than "grasp", because those, who have not previously read the works referred to, as just listed, need, not only to know the names of the works referred to, but also to become familiar with the works themselves.

There is one allusion, in "Mutuality" (MH, p. 45), which I omitted to comment on. Fortunately, Tammy Ho, reviewing *Moving House* for *The Asian Review of Books Online* (24 September 2006), did the job for me. She writes:

> In "Mutuality", the poet articulates the inseparableness of husband and wife:

Communicating Poems

> – Twin trees, closely planted,
> Reach up to the light; reach out to each other.
> One extends, the other yields.
> One sheds leaves, the other roots
> Deeper. The wind blows. They embrace.
> Each other's anchor in the storm.
>
> This stanza from "Mutuality" re-writes and expands on a famous line from a Tang poem about a pair of star-crossed lovers: "In the sky I wish we fly with same wings; on the earth I wish we are trees with roots linked".

The concept of inter-textuality applies also to allusions and debts to other types of works, including works of graphic art. In the poem, "Easter Stunt Man" (MH, p. 55), I refer to a very famous work by nineteenth century British artist Holman Hunt (1827-1910), "The Light of the World" (1851-1853).

Easter Stunt Man

You break out of the egg,
from your three days'
suspension
between life and death;
when the yoke of your mystery
adequately fed on the
protein
of your confidence.

And now you knock at our hearts,
wearing a crown of thorns,
holding a lantern,
for always;
wishing that your *earthly* father,

the *carpenter*,
would come
to fit the door handle
that would let you in.

Cultural References

The notes to the poem, "Easter Stunt Man" (MH, p. 126, n. 9), focus on identifying the inter-textual reference to, "The Light of the World", and on giving some background and commentary on Holman Hunt's painting. Nowhere do I actually explain the basic teachings of Christianity and, clearly, I assume that my readers have some knowledge of Christianity. . . . Should I have been more conscious of addressing a potentially global readership? And should I have attempted some brief explanation of what may be considered a cultural reference, albeit to a major world religion?

As for the <u>content of the notes themselves</u>, should I have identified "Revelations" (MH, p. 126, n. 9) as part of the Christian Bible? Similarly, in the notes to the poem, "Newsworthy", in my earlier collection, *For the Record*, should I have identified St Matthew's Gospel (FTR, p. 118, n. 3) as being from the Holy Bible or, alternatively, should I have provided a gloss on the phrase, "Holy Writ", used in the poem itself? (FTR, p. 38.) In my notes to "Easter Stunt Man" (MH, p. 118, n. 3), should I have explained the contents of the notes themselves? Should I have said who Jesus is and should I have explained that Jesus and Christ are the same (or, instead, should I have used only one term, sacrificing the better style of avoiding such close repetition)?

Certainly, had I provided these additional explanations, some readers would have considered them unnecessary and some would even have been offended at my apparently supposing that "they" did not already know these facts. <u>The expansion of the potential readership for any text, brought</u>

Communicating Poems

by modern technology, has in fact created a dilemma. Of course, not all cultural references are to major world religions, as they are in this poem. But, in each case, whatever the reference, a decision needs to be made as to whether to include an explanation or not. And those who know the information are likely to be critical of its provision as unnecessary or even insulting.

Local references

Another category of references – what may be considered local references – may particularly need explanation, but the selection of the points for comment also requires careful consideration. By what standard can one decide which points most need to be explained?

I have prepared a blank form for readers to give me their own views about this. (Please see below.) If you are interested in doing so, please photo-copy, scan, or type out these two pages (only) for this purpose. and use them to insert your views as to what elements in the three collections, *For the Record and other Poems of Hong Kong, Moving House and other Poems from Hong Kong* and *Sightings* constitute references to a specific (local) culture and/or locality (place), and, if you like, please send me your completed form. Please use the form to indicate, also, whether, if I had consulted you before publication, you would have advised me to include notes in the book explaining each such reference, or not, bearing in mind different possible readerships. If you have time, please also give your reasons for your views, referring to the examples you comment on. Or, if you prefer, please give me your views in general. If you want, you may add your name, email address and phone number to the sheet, but, of course, it is not necessary for you to do this. Please post your reply to the Publisher's address given on the imprint page. The Publisher will not be able to return these to you, so please keep your own copy, if you wish. Please

Communicating Poems

understand that I may not be able to write you a personal reply, but rest assured that I will respond to your views by considering them carefully.

Translation
Translation is of course a long-established means of communicating texts. A translator needs to understand all the points of inter-textuality, local and cultural references, and many more points, in order to do the translation.

Cost of annotation
All the annotations discussed are of course time consuming and expensive, whether in terms of out-of-pocket expenditure or the time involved (the "opportunity cost"). Translation is a particularly expensive exercise (in one or both of these areas). But of course translation is a major means of communication. I will always be very grateful to Dr Simon Sui-cheong Chau, interested particularly in the "green" themes in the book, for translating into Chinese the poems in *For the Record* and to the team who translated *Moving House*. (The team, consisting then (the summer of 2006) of new graduates or undergraduates, all from either Hong Kong Baptist University or the University of Hong Kong, was recruited by Tony Ming-Tak Yip, himself introduced by Dr Ester S. M. Leung, Associate Professor in the Translation Programme of Hong Kong Baptist University.) I now need a translator into Chinese for *Sightings*, this present collection. If any reader is interested in doing this, or in translating one or a few of the poems only, his or her assistance would be very welcome.

Translations into other languages would also be welcomed. The Egyptian novelist and poet, Sayed Gouda, has already translated into Arabic two poems from *Moving House*, which will appear in his, "Anthology of Modern and Contemporary Poetry of China", to be published in

Communicating Poems

Cairo, Egypt, by the Supreme Council of Culture of Egypt, in 2007.

Simplicity of diction and expression
As for the actual writing of the text (as opposed to the presentation of the text for publication, in whatever form), there are well-established conventions for composing such text as is explicitly targeted to a readership of young people and also for composing text explicitly directed to the different target readership of non-native speakers of the language in which the text is written. Given the leading role, which the English language has assumed internationally in recent decades, this is particularly so in the case of texts published in the English language.

But, given that the audience reached for any text will now, in the internet age, include non-native speakers and young people, whether targeted at these readerships or not, should all texts – perhaps, in considering this point, we could limit ourselves to all creative texts – should all creative texts be written with these groups in mind, among other readers?

If writers do this, do write with these groups in mind, among other readers, will the careful simplicity, which is likely to result, be misunderstood as vapidity?

Another answer, or part of an answer, would be to edit out local references. In some cases, I have done this in *Sightings*, the present collection. In any live reading, locally, the original references could perhaps be re-inserted.

Careful editing for the sake of clarity and communicability
It seems there is another danger. Can careful editing of ones own work, for the sake of clarity and communicability, lead to misguided accusations of "insincerity"? – I recently came across this concern in a creative writing class/workshop that I was conducting for adults. One native-speaker participant was concerned at the

idea of editing her own work. "Wouldn't that detract from its sincerity?" she asked.

I personally think that any writer should revise and revise again, polishing their own work as many times as necessary, with communicability as well as elegance of style, expression and meaning as very important considerations.

Surviving manuscripts (MSS) and typescripts (TSS) of many writers and the vast variorum editions of major writers show that this view is not an eccentric one.

Supporting the message with graphics
What about non-text means of conveying the message, added after the text is complete? – Graphic elements such as photos, drawings, collage, paintings, maps, etc? – Some of us are familiar with graphic or concrete poetry. (I myself use it in the present collection, in the last line of "Disappearing Harbour".) It may be found in such different works, far separated in time, as Lewis Carroll's "Fury said to a mouse", which is laid out in the form of a mouse's tail (*Alice's Adventure in Wonderland*),[91] and Anglican divine, George Herbert's "Easter Wings", presented in the form of a pair of open wings (if you turn the page sideways), as shown below.

Communicating Poems

> Lord, Who createdst man in wealth and store,
>   Though foolishly he lost the same,
>   Decaying more and more,
>   Till he became
>   Most poore:
>
>   With Thee
>   O let me rise,
>   As larks, harmoniously,
>   And sing this day Thy victories:
> Then shall the fall further the flight in me.
>
> My tender age in sorrow did beginne:
>   And still with sicknesses and shame
>   Thou didst so punish sinne.
>   That I became
>   Most thinne.
>
>   With Thee
>   Let me combine,
>   And feel this day Thy victorie;
>   For, if I imp my wing on Thine,
> Affliction shall advance the flight in me.[92]

In these examples, however, it seems to me, this graphic feature does not really take the meaning further, although it does <u>underline</u> the meaning. The use of layout, here, exists in its own right. And, in "Easter Wings", at least, it exists as a separate exercise of technical skill.

   In the case of graphics added <u>after</u> the text is complete (rather than as part of the text creation process itself), we may feel that they <u>distract</u> from the meaning, or offer <u>different</u> meanings, even when carefully chosen. One example of a poem in *Moving House and other Poems from Hong Kong*, where graphics could be possible might be:

Communicating Poems

Scene from a Bus II: Sweeping Changes (MH, p. 50)
The street sweeper
uses her mobile phone
standing next to her piled-high trolley.

In the case of, "A Pure Devotion", a drawing or a photograph might be helpful for those not familiar with wayside shrines, such as it describes. Nevertheless, can any reader really not work out the object that is being presented?

A Pure Devotion (MH, p. 79)
It was still there,
the new shrine, that I
first saw yesterday.

The gods had nibbled the biscuits in the
thoughtfully opened packet;

but had left the apples,
wrapped sweets and
oranges,

for another day.

How ones heart is moved!

Pleased at the thought, that
here is offered
thanks for happiness given,

sad in case of
a mute plea
for a need to be met,

warmed
by the possibility
of an absolutely
pure devotion.

Communicating Poems

Is any attempt to illustrate creative literary work in fact misguided? I did consider commissioning illustrations for *Moving House and other Poems from Hong Kong*, but decided, with my consulting editor, that the illustrations we had in mind then would push the poems into secondary importance. Similarly, the editor of *Hong Kong Culture* magazine changed her mind about including a photograph or a drawing, to illustrate a poem from *Moving House*, "Language Lessons", in her March 2006 issue, and used instead a text-based design, quoting from the poem itself. Yet two other issues of *Hong Kong Culture* very successfully illustrate one of my poems in each. In the case of this latest collection, *Sightings*, most of the illustrations do not merely illustrate. Some add an extra dimension of meaning, and some enter into dialogue with the poems themselves. It probably depends on the poem. It may also depend on the extent to which, even with illustrations, there is space for the reader's imagination and intellect to come into play.

Poetry: a special case
All these points of course apply to all texts, particularly all creative texts, not only to poetry. We could go on to ask, is there any way in which poetry is a special case?

Is the spectrum of poetry one where communicability and poeticality are at opposite poles? Is the attempt to communicate an unpoetic objective? Should the poet seek only to express his or her meaning, his or her self; and not seek to communicate with, or to, other people at all?

In earlier days, poetry had only a small audience. The court and city poets of the English Elizabethan and Jacobean periods circulated their poems privately. A comparable situation today exists in Japan (and also, I am sure, elsewhere) where people meet regularly as a group to compose haiku on a subject set by a respected teacher, who will later, during the gathering, comment on the work produced.

Communicating Poems

There are of course large exceptions: for example, in the nineteenth century, Alfred, Lord Tennyson; today, Seamus Heaney. But were or are the large audiences, which the work of these two poets has attracted, an unplanned product of the subjects these writers wrote about and the various styles in which they wrote? Not results deliberately targeted by the writers themselves, at the time of composing their works? . . . It is another maxim of the writing world that, if you target success you will not find it; but that it will come in response to sincerity – that word again! – of work. – Perhaps the answer is different, for each of these two highly popular poets; and the answer may be different also, at different periods of their writing lives.

Conclusion

In reality, however, the decision of whether or not to address vast audiences – both local and global – in a single edition of poetry is out of our hands. Writers, editors and publishers can not limit any utterance – including the contents of an expensive hardbound book – to any particular audience.[93] Both sophisticated and unsophisticated readers can easily take a look at our texts, both in physical form and as uploaded to the internet, with or without our knowledge. (Equally easily, they can express their views about our work, and disseminate them in the same way.) Should we simply hope that they will use the resources of the internet to find out for themselves the information and background that they, individually need?

My own view is that most of those who need additional information will not know what there is that they should be looking for, or how to rephrase and again rephrase the wording they put into the search engines, so as successfully to find the information that they need. I have acted on this view in preparing the present collection, *Sightings*, for publication. I believe that writers and editors – poets and poetry included – are going to need to annotate and explain more and more, even for first publication of any creative work. Hopefully, readers as well as editors and writers, including poets, will come to accept the inclusion of explanations, which many will see as redundant, in the interest of achieving communication.

One final point also refers to poetry in particular and this is the question of reading and performance. Relatively inexperienced or non-native speaking readers (in both senses) would certainly be helped, not necessarily only with preparing a performance, but in understanding the structure of writing, and thus the meaning of the whole, if indications of emphasis, such as italics or underlining are provided. For experienced readers, the pleasure of reading may often partly lie in working out the meaning and creating a performance, for themselves. But it is difficult to put into practice equal consideration for each group. The inclusion of an audio recording of all the poems published in a book is one way of doing this (as in each of *For the Record* and *Moving House*). But this is not always possible; certainly it would be difficult in an anthology, if the plan was to include the voices of the poets themselves. Again, one hopes that the pleasure of experienced and sophisticated readers will not be too much compromised by attempts to reach out to others and, hopefully, to extend their number.

About the Author

Gillian BICKLEY, born and educated in the United Kingdom, has lived mostly in Hong Kong since 1970. Her poetry collections include *For the Record and other Poems of Hong Kong, Moving House, Sightings, China Suite, Perceptions* and the bilingual English-Romanian *Poems*. Two collections – *Moving House* and *For the Record* – have also been published in Chinese; individual poems have been published in Arabic, Catalan, Chinese, Czech, French, German, Romanian, Turkish and other languages. In 2014, she was awarded the "Grand Prix Orient-Occident Des Arts" at the 18th International Festival, "Curtea de Argeș Poetry Nights", held in Romania. Gillian Bickley is one of the Hong Kong poets discussed in Agnes S. L. Lam's study, *Becoming poets: The Asian English Experience*.

Gillian has written or edited several non-fiction books in different fields: *The Golden Needle: The Biography of Frederick Stewart, 1836-1889 (founder of Hong Kong Government Education)*, Hong Kong Baptist University and David C. Lam Institute for East-West Studies, 1997; *Hong Kong Invaded! A '97 Nightmare*, University of Hong Kong Press, Hong Kong, 2001; *The Development of Education in Hong Kong, 1841-1897: as revealed through the Early Education Reports of the Hong Kong Government, 1848-1896*, Proverse Hong Kong, Hong Kong, 2002; *The Stewarts of Bourtreebush*, Centre for Scottish Studies, University of Aberdeen, Scotland, 2003; *A Magistrate's Court in 19th Century Hong Kong: Court in Time*, Proverse Hong Kong, first edition, 2005; second edition, 2009; *The Complete Court Cases of Magistrate Frederick Stewart*, Proverse Hong Kong, 2008; *In Time of War* (in collaboration with Richard Collingwood-Selby), edition based on the writings of the deceased Lieutenant Commander in the Royal Navy, Henry C.S. Collingwood-Selby (1898-1992), Proverse Hong Kong, 2013.

Five of these twelve English-language books received publication support from Hong Kong Arts Development

About the Author

Council (HKADC) and three from Lord Wilson Heritage Trust. The extensive research necessary for six of the non-fiction works listed was made possible by research grants awarded by the Hong Kong Baptist University.

Dr Bickley was Senior Lecturer / Associate Professor in the Department of English at the Hong Kong Baptist University for twenty-two years. She has been a full-time faculty member at the University of Lagos, Nigeria; the University of Auckland, New Zealand; and at the University of Hong Kong.

For several years, Gillian was an adjudicator at the world-famous Hong Kong Schools Music & Speech Associations' annual Speech Festival and has also been a judge for the Budding Poets' Society Hong Kong.

More recently, as co-ordinator of literary activities for a non-profit registered educational charity, she has led reading appreciation sessions which are open to the community and assists to deliver reading courses at local schools. She has worked with the Gifted Education Section of the Education Bureau to encourage creative writing among students. She has completed teaching creative reading / writing courses at the Hong Kong Academy for Gifted Education (HKAGE) and at the University of Hong Kong School for Professional and Continuing Education (HKU SPACE) and lectured on poetry at Lingnan University Community College. Her creative reading / writing course at HKU SPACE continues to be offered. In 2016, she managed twenty and hosted seventeen meet-the-author events at a Hong Kong bookshop.

Following her career in academia, Gillian has become an experienced project-manager, text editor, and production manager, including of poetry, non-fiction, fiction and academic writing.

She has been a member of the Society of Authors in the United Kingdom since her school days.

Notes

Notes

[1] Heartease is a small town in the Parish of Manchester, Jamaica, West Indies. It is also (with its variant, "Heart's ease"), the name of the small pansy, or viola, still used for a variety of medicinal purposes.

[2] The reference is to "Ecclesiastes", chapter 12, verse 12, which reads: "And further, by these, my son, be admonished: of making many books there is no end; and much study is a weariness of the flesh." (King James Version of the Christian Bible) Rightly or wrongly, I seem to have taken this as having a similar meaning to the phrase, "Ars Longa, Vita Brevis" ("Art is long; Life is short"), described in various reference sources as part of an aphorism originating from the Ancient Greek physician, Hippocrates (c. 460 BC - c. 370 BC).

[3] Sigmund Freud (1856-1939) suggested that the "super-ego", composed of internalized norms, morality and taboos, is one of three parts of the human psyche.

[4] The Black Death (bubonic and pneumonic plague) was rampant in West and Central Europe, 1347-1351, with several pandemic recurrences.

[5] Three versions of this miracle are told in the New Testament of the Christian Bible: St Matthew, (9, vi); St Mark (2, xi); St John (5, viii).

[6] Isabella Beeton (1836-1865) wrote *Household Management*, 1859-60.

[7] Squirrels hide nuts away to eat when they wake up from their regular winter hibernation.

[8] In *Hamlet*, IV (v). But it was Mercutio (*Romeo and Juliet*, II, iv), who said, "I am the very pink of courtesy", to which Romeo responded, "pink for flower". Mercutio: "Right".

[9] See Macbeth in, *Macbeth*, II (ii).

[10] This phrase is often used to refer to the training the British traditionally receive, not to betray, or give way to, their emotions.

Notes

[11] William Shakespeare (1564-1616), *Hamlet* (Act IV, scene v). ("There's such divinity doth hedge a king, / That treason can but peep to what it would . . .".)

[12] In Shakespeare's history play, Richard the Second of England was stabbed to death. (See *Richard the Second*, Act V, scene v.)

[13] See Christopher Marlowe (1564-1593), *Edward the Second*, Act V, scene v.

[14] "Discovery" is the name of a type of desert apple. The story of Eve's eating of the apple of the tree of knowledge of Good and Evil, followed by Adam, disobeying God's injunction, and the consequences of their actions, is told in the Christian Bible's Book of Genesis, chapters 2 and 3.

[15] "Paradise Lost", the famous epic poem by English poet, John Milton (1608-1674), states clearly Milton's view that Satan (the devil) was banished from heaven because of his linked sins of discontent and ambition. (The word ambition occurs, usually associated with Satan, in five of the 12 books of the poem (Books 1, 2, 4, 9 and 12). In the poem, Satan seeks to make Eve discontented and ambitious, in her turn, as means of persuading her to disobey God and eat the apple. (See note, above.)

[16] The meanings of "The Word", in this poem are indicated by the following quotation from St John's Gospel of the Christian Bible: "In the beginning was the Word. And the Word was with God. And the Word was God."

[17] Ernest Hemingway's response to F. Scott Fitzgerald's statement, "The rich are different from you and me" was, "Yes, they have more money."

[18] A television documentary showed this custom taking place in Italy.

[19] A Chinese custom at certain festivals, including Ching Ming, the "Grave Sweeping Festival".

[20] For Æneas's visit to the Underworld, which describes such an episode, see Virgil's *Æneid*, Book VI. For an earlier reference to this episode, see Gillian Bickley,

Notes

"Christmas Letters from Afar", in *Moving House and other Poems from Hong Kong*, p. 40.

[21] Legend tells that the Greek musician, Orpheus, descended to the Underworld to try to bring back from death his dear wife, Eurydice, but he failed to observe a condition set by Pluto, God of the Underworld and his attempt did not succeed.

[22] Planchette is a way people have used to try to get in touch with the dead. A group sits in a circle around a table, on the edge of which the letters of the alphabet are arranged. All place a hand on a glass tumbler in the centre of the table. The tumbler may then move in such a way as to point to different letters of the alphabet and thus spell out a message, thought to be from the spirit world. After the First World War, grieving families tried to get in touch with their loved lost sons, killed in the war. Planchette was one of the methods they used. The holding of séances, with mediums, was also popular. T. S. Eliot (1888-1965) describes this activity in his major poem, "The Wasteland". There is renewed interest in such activities whenever there is significant loss of life.

[23] Henry Vaughan, Welsh poet and clergyman, lived from 1621-1695.

[24] Henry Vaughan, "The World", in *Silex Scintillans*, Part I, 1650, line 1.

[25] Henry Vaughan, "They are all gone into the world of light", in *Silex Scintillans*, Part II, 1655, line 1.

[26] Vaughan is buried in Llansantffraed churchyard, Breconshire. The quotation is based on notes made during a personal visit.

[27] In his review of Gillian Bickley, *For the Record and other Poems of Hong Kong*, and referring to Italo Calvino's book, *The City*, Dave McKirdy wrote of "cities of the mind", meaning, our own perceptions of cities we know of, or have known.

[28] Quoted from Verner Bickley, *Poems to Enjoy*, Hong

Notes

Kong, Hong Kong Educational Publishing Co., 1989, Book 1, p. 11.

[29] Experiment suggests that the question means, "Do you want a head massage"? If you do, you should answer, "Yes".

[30] A "cover" in a restaurant means a place setting, i.e. cutlery, crockery, napkin, etc. It can also refer to the covering of clothes.

[31] This idea echoes the eighteenth century idea, in Europe, that modern thinkers, although less impressive than the great thinkers of the past, nevertheless achieved more, intellectually, than "the ancients" did, because they were "standing on their shoulders". The focus here, however, is on the individual(s) who make possible the achievements of others, not those who achieve more because assisted by what others have done. This couplet, seeking to praise an individual (as an "eagle") for making possible the achievements of others, might, unwittingly, offend, if the object of praise identifies with the sparrow rather than the eagle.

[32] The stool is offered as something to stand on in order to reach post office boxes at high level. Normally, one would expect to "use" a key to open such a box.

[33] The story of Noah's Flood is told in the Old Testament of the Christian Bible, in the Book of Genesis. God punishes the inhabitants of the world by sending a flood, which destroys all except Noah and his family. Because of Noah's righteousness, God warns him to prepare an "ark", or a big houseboat, which provides a safe haven during the flood. After being confined in the ark for some time, floating on the flood waters, Noah sends out a dove. The dove returns, with an olive leaf in its bill. This indicates that the flood waters are receding, and that God will give mankind another chance to build their lives in the world.

[34] IFC (The International Finance Centre) is a large complex near the Central Ferry Piers, Hong Kong Island.

Notes

COSCO (China Ocean Shipping (Group) Company) has a large sign on a modern sky-scraper nearby.
[35] White is the colour used for mourning in traditional Chinese culture.
[36] Discovery Bay, Lantau Island, Hong Kong, has a relatively high proportion of non-Chinese among its residents, who travel via Tung Chung to connect with trains and buses to other parts of Hong Kong, or to take flights from the nearby Hong Kong International Airport.
[37] The connection is made through the word, "leaves", which can be made to refer to the pages of a book ("the leaves of a book").
[38] Bonsai is the art by which growing trees or shrubs are carefully and constantly trimmed to inhibit growth and restrict them to miniature size. "Bonsai" also refers to the miniature trees or shrubs themselves.
[39] Harry Ricketts, *People Like Us*, Hong Kong, Eurasia Publishing, 1977.
[40] Commissioned by the Hong Kong Tourism Commission, Hong Kong harbour has been, since early 2006, the scene for a show, combining architectural lighting, laser effects and pyrotechnics, every evening at 8pm.
[41] Placed in Tung Chung new town, Hong Kong, the bench is in fact meant to represent a boat, a reference to Tung Chung's previous life as a fishing village. See "Rowboat", also in *Sightings*.
[42] Philip Larkin (1922-1985), English poet. The poem, "An Arundel Tomb", which is referred to here, first appeared in Larkin's poetry collection, *The Whitsun Weddings*, published in 1964.
[43] Madeleine Marie Slavick, *Delicate Access*, Sixth Finger Press, 2004.
[44] The Trevi Fountain is in Rome, Italy.
[45] Versailles is a magnificent palace outside Paris, France.
[46] "Miss World" is an international beauty pageant.
[47] International Finance Centre Two, is one of the buildings

Notes

a pedestrian may pass through, in Hong Kong, on the way to connect to sea transport to Macau, with its legal casinos. (Hong Kong has no legal casinos, and the only legal gambling is through the Hong Kong Jockey Club.)

[48] These can be seen for sale or in use in many places in Hong Kong. These particular items were seen in a most interesting display at the Pak Tai Temple, Stone Nullah Lane, Hong Kong.

[49] Miss Lesley Hart, a friend of the writer and a public librarian, very kindly researched this lady for the writer, sometime after this poem was first published. One of the pieces of information she kindly sent shows a photograph with the following caption: "Elsie Wood. For many years a familiar and imposing figure as she glided around town, all in white, including her parasol and deathly make-up, and looking neither to left nor right. Her regal perambulations earned her various nicknames such as 'The Woman in White', 'The Queen of Sheba', and 'Queen Mary'. Popular legend told of her having been jilted into the strangeness of her ways." The accompanying photograph, however, dated 10 November 1957, shows Miss Wood wearing mainly black and the caption further comments, "When this photograph was taken (by pure chance) as she waited for a bus near Shrub Hill station, she had more or less forsaken white in favour of black." See also: http://www.worcesternews.co.uk/news/7647606.Colleague_s_recollections_of_Worcester_s_Lady_in_White/

[50] An adjective, based on the name, "Edward". "Edwardian" refers to styles during the reign of King Edward the Seventh of Great Britain (1901-1910).

[51] Cf. "Auguste", the name of the type of circus clown who has his face painted white.

[52] All architectural and place references are to the City of Worcester, in the English Midlands. The Star, The Angel and The Crown are all establishments serving alcoholic liquor, as well as providing rooms to stay.

Notes

[53] Here used as a euphemism for "alcoholic liquor".

[54] "Grey Friars" is a name given to the Franciscans, or Friars Minor, an order founded by St Francis of Assisi. Presumably, "Grey Friars", an old building in the centre of modern Worcester city, was once a Franciscan friary, or had some other relationship to the Franciscans. (The present building dates from c1480. The Dissolution of the Monasteries under King Henry VIII took place in 1536.)

[55] "The Shambles" is a shopping area in Worcester city, previously the area where butchers carried out their business.

[56] Hops (from which beer is made) are a traditional Worcestershire crop.

[57] Meetings of The Society of Friends (members are also called "Quakers") have no set "service" as many other Christian groups have. Members sit in silence and any, who feel inspired to contribute some thoughts, speak up spontaneously. The group opposes war and violence.

[58] Cavaliers and Roundheads wore different styles of clothes, had different hair-styles, spoke differently and worshipped God differently.

[59] Worcester came to be referred to in this way after the two English Civil Wars, because of its loyalty to both Charles I (king, 1625-1649 (when he was executed)) and his son, Charles II (crowned, defeated and fled to France in 1651; restored as king, 1660-1685). Worcester city was first in declaring support for King Charles I and the last to surrender to Cromwell in 1646. The final battle of the second civil war was the Battle of Worcester, 1651, when Charles II was finally defeated.

[60] Ordinary people might go on a tour. A monarch made a "progress" through his or her realm.

[61] "Aperçus" (French), here taken to mean, "perceptions".

[62] The name of a group of twining plants with trumpet-shaped flowers.

[63] The name of an insect.

Notes

[64] Unlike a parasite, which takes nourishment from its host, epiphytes simply perch on their hosts.

[65] Penny-wort is the name given to a group of wild plants with rounded leaves (the shape of a penny coin).

[66] A tom-cat is a male cat.

[67] Clive Viney and Karen Phillipps, *New Colour Guide to Hong Kong Birds* (Hong Kong, Government Printer, 1977, third ed., 1983), suggests that this was possibly a "Great Egret" or "Lesser Egret" (pp. 38-41). However, Viney describes the Great Egret as follows: "Resident. Common on the Mai Po Marshes in winter, less so in summer. In recent years odd pairs have bred annually at Yim Tso Ha or on a nearby island. Occasionally seen elsewhere on migration. . . . Scarce resident in S. China." He describes the Lesser Egret as a "Non-breeding visitor".

[68] "Bentley" and "Mercedes" are the names of two brands of luxury car.

[69] There has been a long association between Scotland and Hong Kong. Important early China merchants include Jardine and Matheson, Scottish gentlemen.

[70] Adapted from, "Men must work and women must weep". (From English writer and clergyman Charles Kingsley's poem, "Three Fishers" (1858).)

[71] The sponge of vinegar is mentioned in three of the four New Testament Gospels. (Matthew, 27, verses 34, 38; Luke, 23, verse 36; John, 19, verse 30.) There is variation in these accounts and in the subsequent discussion of them. This poem does not seek to enter into these discussions. The focus is on the meaning of the crucifixion as a whole; and the verbal link between "sponge" and "expunge" enables movement from one idea to another.

[72] The Grosvenor Museum, Chester, houses the largest collection of Roman tombstones from a single site in Britain. (www.chester.gov.uk/main.asp?page=899)

[73] The first Duke of Westminster (family name, "Grosvenor") donated £4,000 of the £11,000 raised to

Notes

purchase a plot of land for the Museum, which has also, much more recently, benefited from a grant from the Heritage Lottery Fund.

[74] A centurion commanded a group of one hundred men in the Roman army system.

[75] Philip, Duke of Edinburgh, consort of Queen Elizabeth II of Great Britain and Ireland.

[76] Charles, Prince of Wales.

[77] Somerset and Cornwall are two rural counties in the south of England.

[78] James Abbott McNeill Whistler (1834-1903), American expatriate painter.

[79] Actually, it was Whistler's painting, *Nocturne in Black and Gold: The Falling Rocket,* not this painting, which Ruskin attacked as described a few lines below. Whistler sued Ruskin for libel and won the case. However, the minute damages awarded to Whistler indicate that the sympathies of the court were for Ruskin.

[80] John Ruskin (1819-1900), English poet and essayist, art critic and collector.

[81] Actually, the costs awarded to Whistler were even less, a farthing.

[82] "To serve time" refers to a term in prison; here of course used metaphorically.

[83] Whistler's painting, "The Woman in White" is now in the Freer Gallery, Washington, DC.

[84] The Italian writer, Carlo Collodi (1826-1890), wrote the children's novel, *The Adventures of Pinocchio,* published 1881-1883. The "hero" is the wooden puppet, Pinocchio, and the carver who made the puppet, in the story, is Guiseppe.

[85] See Carla Emery, "Svengali", in, *Don't Tell: The Encyclopedia of Hypnotism.* Can be seen at: hypnotism.org/Svengali.htm@CarlaEmery.

[86] In western usage, the word, "butterfly", can be used to refer to a frivolous or inconstant person.

Notes

[87] Diners Club is an international credit card.
[88] *Sic*.
[89] The phoenix, a mythical bird, is capable of regeneration from its own ashes.
[90] Gillian Bickley, *Moving House and other Poems from Hong Kong*. Hong Kong: Proverse Hong Kong, 2005, p. 125, n. 6.
[91] Example offered by Verner Bickley.
[92] George Herbert's dates are 1593-1633. "Imp" means, "graft", a term from falconry.
[93] Even closed archives come into the public domain after a set number of years, and even though their complete understanding requires specialized experience and knowledge, this does not prevent published work appearing that comments on their contents.

From Advance Comments and Reviews of Published Poetry by Gillian Bickley

Sightings

"Gillian Bickley's verse is often remarkable for its economy and breath-taking delicacy. It ranges from reactions to the interface of technology and nature to the simple facts of being a student, teacher or writer. The forms are daring and varied, the images potent and memorable yet, through all the verse there is a sense of deep interest in and compassion for humanity. Illustrations and an insightful essay on the communication of poetry enhance this volume and make it much more than a collection of poems. Rather, it is a celebration and investigation of what poetry can, and in this case, does do supremely well...."
—Ken Pickering. Professor: The Institute for Arts in Therapy and Education: London

Perceptions

"*Perceptions* has a vivid personal touch, characteristically descriptive of the poet's experiences and sensations as well as a unique sense of time.... I am particularly struck by the poet's empathies to many common issues. The people, the places, the issues, the sentiments and all become a texture that is so tangible to feel and to smell." —Chan Yee Shan

"*Perceptions* is a treasure house of contemporary writing.
Its poems and short pieces span over time and space, straddling Albania, the Pyrenees, Nigeria, Hong Kong and other places.

Humourously, philosophically, the book covers subjects of survival, love, relationship with other species and various human conditions and lifestyles.

There is a common thread which wends throughout these pieces in search of a higher social order and in finding the value of self-identification.

From the book, [the poem 'Legs'] provides an appropriate representative illustration of a contemporary poetic style. Intense in feeling and simple in expression, the poem uses an ordinary theme to trigger thoughts of deeper conflict in life. Its unique paragraphing and punctuations form an essential part of the poetic expression...."
—From a bilingual (English/Chinese) review by Libby Wong, *MingPao*, 10 September 2014.

China Suite

"Gillian Bickley's *China Suite and Other Poems* is a collection refined by the sensitivity and spirit of a poet who observes with the wonder and clarity of someone who is at once an insider and outsider.... In her works, we see that Bickley's poetry has the ability to provide both spontaneous, on-the-spot immediacy and lingering, contemplative power...."

— Hilary Chan Tsz-Shan, Reviews, *Asian Cha*, February 2010 (Issue 10).

"Every city may have its gaps, ambiguities and unknowabilities, and the poet's intimate and candid reflections in this collection have successfully uncovered some of them."

— Hilary Chan Tsz-Shan (as above)

Moving House and other Poems from Hong Kong

"Images, as if from a poetic camera, of experiences and reflections of existence in Hong Kong." "The poetic observations of a sensitive writer responding to the reality of being alive." "Insightful probing into the darker issues of our lives . . . to make sense of human experience." — Paul Bench, *Speech & Drama: Journal of the Society of Teachers of Speech and Drama*.

"A privileged view into the emotional, intellectual and spiritual life of its writer." "The profound intimacy of the personal poems, reflecting universal truths about the human condition, renders the reader at once intruder and confidant." — Solveig Bang, *Sunday Morning Post*, Hong Kong.

"Bickley's delicately-crafted poems are faithful word portraits of various aspects of Hong Kong at the turn of the millennium: its landscape, its people, its myths and spirits."
— Tammy Ho, *Asian Review of Books*.

"Bickley emerges from the poems as a funny, perceptive, caring, and wise person." "Adventurous in scope." "Much of the poetry is easy access — poems that strip themselves bare for the reader". — MM, *Hong Kong Magazine*.

"Gillian Bickley writes as she responds to everyday events, always with the echo of 'time's wingèd chariot' in her ears. The variety of human life and the individual response to life, these are Gillian Bickley's central interests. In this bare, tight poetry, no idle words are allowed. Its vocabulary draws on the base language of essences and epiphanies. The chosen spare language is the perfect partner for this poetry of mature experience."
— Emeritus Professor I. F. Clarke and M. Clarke, UK.

***Moving House* and *For the Record*, taken together**
"Fresh, insightful and in rhythm with the sensitivities of a community passing through a period of political and social change." "An important contribution to the evolution of cross-cultural poetry in, and about, Hong Kong." "Some of her reflective pieces are thought provoking, even challenging." "Perhaps at her best in describing people and commonplace events in Hong Kong." "She paints a rich and textured canvas." "Shared humility and humanity."
— Ian Wotherspoon, *The Overseas Pensioner*, UK.

For the Record and other Poems of Hong Kong

"Thought-provoking and entertaining." "Not even the American minimalist William Carlos Williams could zero in on and capture a detail with more panache." "Bickley succeeds in conveying the character of the Fragrant Harbour with humorous rigour." — David Wilson, *Sunday Morning Post*, HK.

"She skillfully fuses the human and the natural world." — David McKirdy, *Asian Review of Books*.

"A perceptive account of life and people mostly in Hong Kong, rendered with empathy, humour and surprise." — Agnes Lam.

"Gillian Bickley's version of Hong Kong is based on the knowledge gained as a long-term resident. She puts her findings on the record." — Andrew Parkin, Paris.

"The poet's presence is tangible throughout, from poems on materialism to marriage, and expatriate life to the 1997 'handback — not Handover — to China'." — Madeleine Marie Slavick.

"I had difficulty putting it down. In Bickley's own inimitable style." — Dr Dan Waters, author of *One Couple Two Cultures*.

"Bickley's work is fun to read. She is an expatriate, but sometimes with a local perspective." — Cindy Yik-Yi Chu, *Hong Kong Journal of Modern Chinese History*.

WRITE TO US!

We are interested to read your comments on
Gillian Bickley's *Sightings*.
Write to our email address, giving us a few sentences
which you are willing for us to publish,
describing your response to this book.
If your comments are chosen to be included
in our E-Newsletter or website,
we will select another title published by Proverse
and send you a complimentary copy.
Please include your name, email address and mailing
address when you write to us, and state whether or not we
may cut or edit your comments for publication.
We will use your initials to attribute your comments.

POETRY PUBLISHED BY PROVERSE

Chasing Light, by Patricia Glinton Meicholas. 2013.

China Suite and other Poems, by Gillian Bickley. 2009.

For the Record and other Poems of Hong Kong, by Gillian Bickley, 2003.

Frida Kahlo's Cry and other Poems, by Laura Solomon. 2015.

Home, Away, Elsewhere, by Vaughan Rapatahana. 2011.

Immortelle and Bhandaaraa Poems, by Lelawattee Manoo-Rahming. 2011.

In Vitro, by Laura Solomon. 2nd ed. 2013.

Irreverent Poems for Pretentious People, by Henrik Hoeg. 2016.

Moving House and other Poems from Hong Kong, by Gillian Bickley. 2005.

Of Symbols Misused, by Mary-Jane Newton. March 2011.

Painting the Borrowed House: Poems, by Kate Rogers. 2008.

Perceptions, by Gillian Bickley. 2012.

Rain on the Pacific Coast, by Elbert Siu Ping Lee. 2013.

refrain, by Jason S. Polley. 2010.

Shadow Play, by James Norcliffe. 2012.

Shadows in Deferment, by Birgit Bunzel Linder. 2013.

Shifting Sands, by Deepa Vanjani. 2016.

Sightings: a collection of poetry, with an essay, 'communicating poems', by Gillian Bickley. 2007.

Smoked pearl: Poems of Hong Kong and Beyond, by Akin Jeje (Akinsola Olufemi Jeje). 2010.

The Burning Lake, by Jonathan Hart. Scheduled November 2016.

Unlocking, by Mary-Jane Newton. 2013.

Wonder, Lust & Itchy feet, by Sally Dellow. 2011.

POETRY – CHINESE LANGUAGE

For the record and other poems of Hong Kong, by Gillian Bickley. Translated by Simon Chow. 2010. E-bk.

Moving House and other poems from Hong Kong, translated into Chinese, with additional material, by Gillian Bickley. Edited by Tony Ming-Tak Yip. Translated by Tony Yip & others. 2008.

~~~

**FIND OUT MORE ABOUT OUR AUTHORS
BOOKS, EVENTS AND INTERNATIONAL PRIZES**

Visit our website
http://www.proversepublishing.com
Visit our distributor's website
<www.chineseupress.com>

Follow us on Twitter
Follow news and conversation:
<twitter.com/Proversebooks>
OR
Copy and paste the following to your browser window and follow the instructions:
https://twitter.com/#!/ProverseBooks

"Like" us on www.facebook.com/ProversePress
Request our E-Newsletter
Send your request to info@proversepublishing.com.

Availability
Most titles are available in Hong Kong and world-wide from our Hong Kong based Distributor,
The Chinese University Press of Hong Kong,
The Chinese University of Hong Kong, Shatin, NT,
Hong Kong SAR, China. Web: chineseupress.com

All titles are available from Proverse Hong Kong and the Proverse Hong Kong UK-based Distributor. We have stock-holding retailers in Hong Kong, Singapore (Select Books), Canada (Elizabeth Campbell Books), Principality of Andorra (Llibreria La Puça, La Llibreria). Orders can be made from bookshops in the UK and elsewhere.

Ebooks: Most of our titles are available also as Ebooks.

www.ingramcontent.com/pod-product-compliance
Lightning Source LLC
Chambersburg PA
CBHW070938180426
43192CB00039B/2325